TO
NANCY AND M:

HANG on to
someday it could be
worth $11.95

Sheldon
Cooper

JONAS WILKERSON WAS A GRAVY-SUCKIN' PIG

& OTHER TRIVIAL FACTS

LUDLOW PORCH

LONGSTREET PRESS
Atlanta, Georgia

Published by
LONGSTREET PRESS, INC.
2150 Newmarket Parkway
Suite 102
Marietta, Georgia 30067

Printed in the United States of America

1st Printing, 1988

Library of Congress Catalog Card Number 88-081801

ISBN 0-929264-04-5

This book was printed by R. R. Donnelley and Sons, Harrisonburg, Virginia. The text type was set in Times Roman by Typo-Repro Service, Inc., Atlanta, Georgia. Design by Paulette Lambert. Cover photo by Robert Hill.

Dedication

*To Phil and Charlie
Two great trivia players
and two great sons*

Special Thanks

*It has been my great good fortune over the years to
hang out with some of the world's best trivia
players. Some of them have made this book possible.
They have furnished questions, encouragement, and,
on some occasions, whiskey. My special love and
thanks to:*

*Hank (The Prank) Morgan
Stuart Lewengrub
Bill Sanders
Phil Hanson
Gil Campbell
Charlie McGarvey
Randy Schmidt*

and to Connie Pope.

Other books by Ludlow Porch

A View from the Porch

The Cornbread Chronicles

There's Nothing Neat About Seeing Your Feet

*Can I Just Do It Till I Need Glasses? and Other Lies
Grown-ups Told You*

Weirdos, Winos & Defrocked Priests

Who Cares About Apathy?

Contents

Foreword

Trivia should be played only for fun. Lord save me from the folks who take it too seriously. I have known people to risk stroke by getting in an uproar over one little trivia question. That's not the way I play.

For years, in a newspaper feature and on my radio show, I have played trivia with my readers and listeners. This book is a summary of those years of enjoyment and challenge. I picked my favorite trivia subjects, and I've tried to arrange the book so that beginners and experts alike can have a good time with it. Some chapters, such as the television section, have general questions on M*A*S*H or westerns appropriate for trivia novices. For the hard-core players, there are extended special sections on certain subjects, such as the *Andy Griffith Show* and cowboys, to let them show off a little, all in good fun, of course.

When the game Trivial Pursuit first came out, some people got bent out of shape about some mistakes in the answers. I may have made some mistakes myself. If I have, let me know through my publisher. We'll fix 'em. But that's another nice thing about trivia: it's trivial. Don't get mad. Get smart (remember?—Don Adams, Agent 99, the Chief). Have fun.

Tuning in to America's Favorite Pastime

Some people call television a wasteland. Others say it's the boob tube. Me? I figure TV is like most anything else—some trash, some jewels, and a lot of stuff in between.

For the purposes of trivia, though, it's hard to argue that the magic box doesn't provide a wealth of questions to tease the brain and, in some cases, make us long for the good old days of *Dragnet* (when cops wore badges and sensible suits, not fuchsia jackets they forgot to get pressed) and *Perry Mason* (where right was right and Perry set things straight).

See how much you remember. Warning: couch potatoes have an unfair advantage in this section.

1. Who was Bolivar Shagnasty?

2. Can you remember the name of Sky King's airplane?

3. What was the full name of the Dobie Gillis show?

4. Who was Luke's wife on *The Real McCoys*?

5. What was Chief Ironside's first name?

6. Name Dobie Gillis's hometown.

7. On the TV series, what was Annie Oakley's horse named?

8. What was Annie Oakley's brother's name?

9. Name the dog on *The Brady Bunch*.

10. Who was the best friend of Dennis the Menace?

11. Who was the teacher on television's *Ding Dong School*?

12. Name Columbo's wife.

13. Who starred in the short-lived series *Saints and Sinners*?

14. Casper, the Friendly Ghost, had a horse; can you name her?

15. What was the name of the town closest to the Rifleman's ranch?

16. Who was the only left-handed Cartwright?

17. On *Star Trek*, what was Dr. McCoy's first name?

18. Name Yogi Bear's sidekick.

1. A Red Skelton character

2. The *Songbird*

3. *The Many Loves of Dobie Gillis*

4. Kate

5. Robert

6. Springfield

7. Target

8. Tagg

9. Tiger

10. Tommy Anderson

11. Miss Frances

12. Mildred

13. Nick Adams

14. Nightmare

15. North Fork

16. Little Joe

17. Leonard

18. Boo Boo

19. What was the name of the station-house dog on *Emergency*?

20. Name Roy Rogers's dog.

21. On what national TV show did Elvis Presley make his television debut?

22. What was Festus's mule named on *Gunsmoke*?

23. Two actors played Steve Wilson on *Big Town*; can you name them?

24. On *Hawaii Five-O* what is Steve McGarrett's middle name?

25. Who played Peter Gunn?

26. Who is Frances Octavia Smith?

27. Who is Eunice Quedens?

28. Name Tonto's horse.

29. Who was Vint Bonner?

30. What was the theme song of *The Three Stooges*?

31. Who played Hopalong Cassidy on TV?

32. Who played Mark on *The Rifleman*?

33. What was the theme song of *The Jeffersons*?

34. Who was Hazel's TV boss?

35. Who was John F. Sullivan?

36. What was Joe Friday's badge number on *Dragnet*?

19. Boots

20. Bullet

21. *A Stage Show*, starring Jimmy and Tommy Dorsey (January 28, 1956)

22. Ruth

23. Mark Stevens and Patrick McVey

24. Aloysius

25. Craig Stevens

26. Dale Evans

27. Eve Arden

28. Scout

29. John Payne in *The Restless Gun*

30. Three Blind Mice

31. William Boyd

32. Johnny Crawford

33. "Movin' On Up"

34. Mr. Baxter

35. Real name of Fred Allen

36. 714

37. Name the creator of *Star Trek*.

38. Name the actor who played Sergeant Preston of the Yukon.

39. Who was the Tennessee Plowboy?

40. What is Steve Allen's theme song?

41. Do you remember the name of the Millionaire's estate?

42. Name the character who played Jimmy Olson on *Superman*.

43. Alan Hale, Jr., was the TV sidekick of what famous cowboy?

44. Who is Herbert B. Khaury?

45. From *Roots*, what was Kunta Kinte's slave name?

46. What does Tony the Tiger advertise on TV?

47. Who was Topo Gigio?

48. Name the dog on *My Three Sons*.

49. Name Zorro's black TV horse.

50. Who owned Mr. Ed?

51. What was Mr. Peepers's first name?

52. What were the first names of Mr. and Mrs. North?

53. Who was Buffy Davis?

54. Where did Archie Bunker work?

37. Gene Roddenberry

38. Richard Simmons

39. Eddy Arnold

40. "This Could Be the Start of Something Big"

41. Silverstone

42. Jack Larkin

43. Gene Autry

44. Tiny Tim

45. Toby

46. Kellogg's Sugar-Frosted Flakes

47. The mouse that spoke with a thick Italian accent on the *Ed Sullivan Show*

48. Tramp

49. Tornado

50. Wilbur Post

51. Robinson

52. Pam and Jerry

53. The little girl in *Family Affair* played by Anissa Jones

54. The Prendergast Tool & Dye Company

55. Can you name the Jeffersons' doorman?

56. On *Batman*, who played the Riddler?

57. Name Red Skelton's famous seagulls.

58. Who was Roy Coffee?

59. Name Sergeant Preston of the Yukon's lead sled dog.

60. Name Clark Kent's hometown.

61. What is Kermit T. Frog's middle name?

62. Who played Davy Crockett on TV?

63. What was Barney Fife's middle name?

64. Name Dennis the Menace's father and mother.

65. What was the buzzer on *Truth or Consequences* called?

66. Can you name Lawrence Welk's theme song?

67. Who was Dan Reed?

68. Who sang the theme song for *Baretta*?

69. Who was the announcer on the *Perry Como Show*?

70. Who was known as the Queen of the Super Circus?

71. What year did *Alfred Hitchcock Presents* first appear on TV?

72. Who was the narrator on *The Untouchables*?

73. Name the author of the book *Lassie Come Home*?

55. Ralph, played by Ned Wertimer

56. Frank Gorshin

57. Gertrude and Heathcliffe

58. The sheriff on *Bonanza*

59. King—his full name was Yukon's King

60. Smallville, Illinois

61. The

62. Fess Parker

63. Oliver

64. Henry and Alice Mitchell

65. Beulah the Buzzer

66. "Bubbles in the Wine"

67. The Lone Ranger's nephew

68. Sammy Davis, Jr.

69. Frank Gallop

70. Mary Hartline

71. 1955

72. Walter Winchell

73. Eric Knight

74. Who played Dan August on TV?

75. Edward R. Murrow had a hit television show in 1951. Name it.

76. Who played Annie Oakley?

77. Who played Dennis the Menace?

78. Who was the host of *Beat the Clock*?

79. Who does the voice of Bugs Bunny?

80. Who played Tarzan in the TV series?

81. Who was Dudley Do-Right's sweetheart?

82. What was the Saint Bernard's name on *Topper*?

83. Who starred in *The Third Man*?

84. Who was billed as America's Favorite Flying Cowboy?

85. Who was Dan Matthews?

86. In what year was *Tom Corbett, Space Cadet* set?

87. Who played Ethel Mertz on *I Love Lucy*?

88. Who played Fred Mertz?

89. Name the 1976 movie based on the hit TV series *Peter Gunn*.

90. Name the actor who played Perry White on *Superman*.

91. Who is David Yarmy?

74. Burt Reynolds

75. *See It Now*

76. Gail Davis

77. Jay North

78. Bud Collyer

79. Mel Blanc

80. Ron Ely

81. Nell Fenwick

82. Neal

83. Michael Rennie

84. Sky King

85. Broderick Crawford's character on *Highway Patrol*

86. 2355

87. Vivian Vance

88. William Frawley

89. *Gunn*

90. John Hamilton

91. Real name of actor Don Adams

92. Who is Sara Jane Fulks?

93. What was the name of our Miss Brooks's landlady?

94. On *The Ghost and Mrs. Muir*, where did Mrs. Muir live?

95. Name the home of Wonder Woman.

96. Name the Beaver's hometown.

97. Name the hospital where Dr. Marcus Welby sent his patients.

98. In *Gunsmoke*, what was Chester's last name?

99. Who was Al Munday?

100. In the TV commercials, who was Ben Gay's archenemy?

101. What was the last name of the family in *Bachelor Father*?

102. Where did the Cartwright family live?

103. Who was Dick Grayson?

104. In *McMillan and Wife*, what was McMillan's first name?

105. Who played Kate on *The Real McCoys*?

106. To what precinct was Barney Miller assigned?

107. Who was the star of *Racket Squad*?

108. Who sponsored *The $64,000 Question*?

109. On *Wagon Train*, what was Major Adams's first name?

92. Real name of Jane Wyman

93. Mrs. Davis

94. Gull Cottage

95. Paradise Island

96. Mayfield

97. Lang Memorial

98. Goode

99. Robert Wagner in *To Catch a Thief*

100. Peter Pain

101. Gregg

102. On the Ponderosa Ranch (two thousand square miles) near Virginia City, Nevada

103. Robin, the Boy Wonder

104. Stewart

105. Kathy Nolan

106. 12th precinct

107. Reed Hadley

108. Revlon

109. Seth

110. Name the butler on *The Addams Family*.

111. Who was our Miss Brooks's boyfriend?

112. Who was Frank Ballinger?

113. Name Dobie Gillis's best friend.

114. From the *Jack Benny Show*, what was Rochester's last name?

115. Who was Sam O'Brian?

116. Who played Pete on *Pete & Gladys*?

117. What did they call the bleachers where the children sat on *The Howdy Doody Show*?

118. On *The Beverly Hillbillies*, what was Jethro's last name?

119. On *Perry Mason*, what was Lieutenant Tragg's first name?

120. From the land of TV commercials, name the Pepsi Twins.

121. Who was the host of *I've Got a Secret*?

122. Who said, "Well, I'll be a dirty bird"?

123. Who said, "Here he is, the one, the only, Groucho"?

124. What was Bullwinkle's full name?

125. Who was Bud Collyer's assistant on *Beat the Clock*?

126. On *Rin Tin Tin*, what company was Rusty in?

110. Lurch

111. Philip Boynton

112. Lee Marvin's character on *M Squad*

113. Maynard G. Krebs (Maynard said the *G* stood for Walter)

114. Van Jones

115. The bartender at the Longbranch Saloon on *Gunsmoke*

116. Harry Morgan

117. The Peanut Gallery

118. Bodine

119. Arthur

120. Pepsi and Peat

121. Garry Moore

122. George Gobel

123. George Fenneman

124. Bullwinkle J. Moose

125. Roxanne

126. B Company

127. Who played Klinger on *M*A*S*H*?

128. In what county is *Hee Haw* set?

129. Who played Chico on *Chico and the Man*?

130. What was the theme song on the *Burns & Allen Show*?

131. What was Lucy Ricardo's maiden name?

132. On TV, where did Rin Tin Tin live?

133. On *Hogan's Heroes*, who was Commandant Klink's superior officer?

134. Name Howdy Doody's sister.

135. What is the theme song of the *Tonight Show*?

136. Where did Dr. Kildare work?

137. Where did Ben Casey work?

138. Who was the announcer on *Ted Mack's Original Amateur Hour*?

139. On *The Beverly Hillbillies*, what was Granny's name?

140. What was the first *Peanuts* show on television?

141. Who played Riley's wife on *The Life of Riley*?

142. Who was Donna Mullenger?

143. Who played the title role in *Wild Bill Hickok*?

144. Can you name Sergeant Preston of the Yukon's horse?

127. Jamie Farr

128. Kornfield Kounty

129. Freddie Prinz

130. "Love Nest"

131. Lucille McGillicuddy

132. Fort Apache

133. General Burkhalter

134. Heidi Doody

135. "Here's Johnny"

136. Blair General Hospital

137. County General Hospital

138. Dennis James

139. Daisy Moses

140. *A Charlie Brown Christmas*

141. Rosemary DeCamp the first year, Marjorie Reynolds after that

142. Donna Reed

143. Guy Madison

144. Rex

145. Name the Indian tribe in *F-Troop*.

146. What was the name of Pat Brady's Jeep?

147. Name the Walton family's hound.

148. Who is Milton Hines?

149. Where were *Hogan's Heroes* held captive?

150. Who was José Melis?

151. Who was Lee Hobson?

152. From *Gunsmoke*, what was Miss Kitty's last name?

153. Yogi Bear was the most famous resident of Jellystone Park. What was the name of the park ranger?

154. Who was Joey Stivic?

155. Who was Johnny Yuma?

156. Who was the elevator operator in *Make Room for Daddy*?

157. Who played Josephine, the Plumber, in the Comet commercials?

158. On *Baretta*, where did Tony Baretta live?

159. What was Kojak's first name?

160. Who is Eugene Orowitz?

161. What year did *Laugh-In* first appear on TV?

162. What are the first names of the Lennon Sisters?

145. Hekawi

146. Nellie Belle

147. Reckless

148. Soupy Sales

149. Stalag 13

150. Jack Parr's bandleader

151. One of the Untouchables

152. Russell

153. John Smith

154. Archie Bunker's grandson

155. Lead character in *The Rebel*

156. José Jiménez (played by Bill Dana)

157. Atlanta native Jane Withers

158. The King Edward Hotel—his rent was $90 a month

159. Theodore

160. Michael Landon

161. 1968—yes, indeed, it's been twenty years

162. Dianne, Peggy, Janet and Kathy

This film beauty went on to become Mrs. Herman Munster. Can you name her?

Yvonne de Carlo

This lady starred in one of TV's longest running series. Name her.

Amanda Blake (Miss Kitty on *Gunsmoke*)

Television Themes

Even bad television shows can have great themes. Some TV themes have been good enough to become hit songs in their own right. There's hardly a person in America who can't sing at least one for you and surely everybody would be able to say *Bonanza* or *The Flintstones* if you hummed a few bars. Let's see how carefully you've been listening all these years.

1. Name the principal orchestra conductors on the following late-night network TV programs:

   A. *Broadway Open House with Jerry Lester*

   B. *The Jack Paar Show* (I and II)

   C. *The Tonight Show with Steve Allen*

   D. *The Tonight Show with Johnny Carson*

2. What was the title and who sang the theme for the TV show *Baretta*?

3. Name the title of the theme from *M*A*S*H*.

4. Name the title of the theme from *The Naked City*.

5. What popular big band played *The Mod Squad* theme on TV?

1. A. Milton DeLugg

    B. Josè Melis

    C. Skitch Henderson

    D. Doc Severinsen

2. "Keep Your Eye On the Sparrow"; Sammy Davis, Jr.

3. *Suicide is Painless*, by Johnny Mandel

4. *Somewhere in the Night*, by Billy May and Milton Raskin

5. Count Basie

6. Name the closing theme song sung by the star on *The Milton Berle Show*.

7. What popular vocalist composed and sang the theme for TV's *Chico and the Man?*

8. Name the theme from *Laverne and Shirley*.

9. Name the theme from *Dragnet*.

10. What popular country-and-western star wrote and sang the opening theme on TV's *Movin' On?*

11. Name the theme from *The Beverly Hillbillies*.

12. Name the theme from *The Roy Rogers Show*.

13. Name the opening and closing themes on *Your Lucky Strike Hit Parade*.

14. Name the theme from *You Bet Your Life* with Groucho Marx.

15. Name the theme from the *Glen Campbell Goodtime Hour*.

16. What orchestra leader composed and conducted the theme from *The Red Skelton Show?*

17. Name the theme from *The Gene Autry Show*.

18. What popular vocalist sang the opening theme from *Rawhide?*

19. Name the theme from *The Dave Garroway Show*.

20. Name the theme from *The Bell Telephone Hour*.

21. Name the theme from *The Green Hornet*.

22. Name the theme from *I Remember Mama*.

6. "Near You," by Francis Craig

7. José Feliciano

8. "Making Our Dreams Come True," by Cyndi Gresse

9. "The Dragnet March" (aka "Danger Ahead")

10. Merle Haggard

11. "The Ballad of Jed Clampett," by Lester Flatt and Earl Scruggs

12. "Happy Trails," by Dale Evans

13. Opening: "Lucky Day"; closing: "So Long for Awhile"

14. "Hooray for Captain Spalding," by Bert Kalmar and Harry Ruby

15. "Gentle on My Mind," by John Hartford

16. David Rose ("Holiday for Strings")

17. "Back in the Saddle Again," by Gene Autry and Ray Whitely

18. Frankie Laine

19. "Sentimental Journey," by Les Brown and Bud Green

20. "The Bell Waltz," by Don Voorhees

21. "The Flight of the Bumble Bee," played by Al Hirt

22. Greig's Halverg Suite, "The Last Spring"

23. Name the orchestra leaders on the following popular TV shows:

   A. *The Ed Sullivan Show*

   B. *The Arthur Godfrey Show and Talent Scouts*

   C. *The Perry Como Show*

   D. *The Merv Griffin Show*

   E. *Route 66*

   F. *Stop the Music*

24. What orchestra leader composed and conducted the "Theme from Peter Gunn"?

25. Name the musical theme for *The Bob Hope Show*.

26. Name the musical theme for *The Jack Benny Show*.

27. Name the musical theme for *The Andy Williams Show*.

28. Name the musical theme for *The Danny Thomas Show*.

29. Name the musical theme for *The Donna Reed Show*.

23.   A. Ray Bloch

B. Archie Bleyer

C. Mitchell Ayres

D. Mort Lindsay

E. Nelson Riddle

F. Harry Sosnick

24.   Henry Mancini

25.   "Thanks for the Memory," by Leo Robin and Ralph Rainger

26.   "Love in Bloom," by Leo Robin and Ralph Rainger

27.   "Moon River," by Henry Mancini and Johnny Mercer

28.   "Danny Boy" (traditional Irish ballad)

29.   "Happy Days"

The
Andy Griffith
Show

In my opinion, *The Andy Griffith Show* was far and away the best thing ever shown on TV. There are several reasons for the success of the show.

The characters were well developed, funny and very, very human.

The scripts were well done, and the actors were wonderful.

I think, however, that the town of Mayberry, North Carolina, was the real reason for its great success. Deep down in my heart, I wish Mayberry was my hometown.

I think most Americans feel the same way.

1. What was Andy Taylor's middle name?

2. What church did he attend?

3. Besides being sheriff, what other job did Andy have?

4. What did Andy call his prized fishing rod?

5. What was Barney's middle name?

6. In what branch of the military did Andy serve?

7. In what branch of the military did Barney serve?

8. Who is Opie's godfather?

9. Where did Andy and Barney go to high school?

1. Jackson

2. All Souls Church, later called the Community Church

3. He was Justice of the Peace

4. Eagle-eye Annie

5. During the course of the series, three middle names are given for Barney: Milton, Oliver, and P.

6. He was in the Army and served in France during WWII.

7. He was in the Army. During his tour, he was stationed at the Staten Island PX library.

8. Barney

9. Mayberry Union High (however, in one episode, called Mayberry Central High)

10. What was Thelma Lou's last name?

11. Name the town drunk.

12. Who owned the gas station?

13. Name the drugstore.

14. What did Howard Sprague do for a living?

15. Who ran the Fixit Shop?

16. Who replaced Barney as deputy?

17. Who was the best rock-thrower in the county?

18. What was Mr. Darling's first name?

19. Who was Mr. Darling's only daughter?

20. Name the *Andy Griffith Show* theme song.

21. During the course of the show, Mayberry had two mayors. Can you name them?

22. Who is Opie's best friend?

23. Who was Howard Sprague's girlfriend?

24. Who was Andy's pastor?

25. Who was Howard's stepfather?

26. Who are Gomer's two favorite actors?

27. Who bought Wally's gas station?

28. What kind of gasoline did Wally sell?

29. Where was the gas station located?

10. It was never given.

11. Otis Campbell

12. Wally

13. Walker's Drugstore

14. County Clerk

15. Emmett Clark

16. Warren Ferguson

17. Ernest T. Bass

18. Briscoe

19. Charlene

20. "The Fishin' Hole"

21. Mayor Pike and Mayor Roy Stoner

22. Johnny Paul Jason

23. Millie Hutchins

24. The Reverend Hobart Tucker

25. George Watkins

26. John Wayne and Preston Foster

27. Goober

28. Acme

29. The intersection of Main and Garden

30. What is Aunt Bee's home state?

31. Where did Aunt Bee go to school?

32. What was Leon's favorite sandwich?

33. Name Opie's dog.

34. What was Mayberry's best-known grocery store?

35. Name the members of the Mayberry bowling team.

36. What lucky fisherman finally caught the famous silver carp, Old Sam?

37. What is Howard's favorite band?

38. What is Howard's favorite drink?

39. What is Goober's last name?

40. What is Floyd's last name?

41. Who was the best guitar player in the county?

42. What band did he play with?

43. How much did Barney weigh?

44. Where did Gomer live?

45. What is Helen Crump's home state?

46. What is Thelma Lou's home phone number?

47. Who was the first woman on the Mayberry Town Council?

48. What does Otis Campbell do for a living?

49. What instrument does Floyd play in the town band?

30. West Virginia

31. Sweetbriar Normal School

32. Peanut butter and jelly

33. Gulliver

34. Foley's Grocery

35. Andy, Howard, Goober and Emmett

36. Howard Sprague

37. The Silver Herringbones

38. Root beer

39. Pyle (in some early episodes, Beasley)

40. Lawson (in at least one episode, Colby)

41. Jim Lindsey

42. Freddy Fleet and His Band with a Beat (also called Bobby Fleet and His Band with a Beat)

43. His weight is given at various times as 100, 132 and 138 pounds.

44. In a room in the back of Wally's Service Station

45. Kansas

46. 247

47. Ellie May Walker

48. Glue dipper at the furniture factory

49. Trumpet

50. Who is the leader of the town band?

51. Who was Floyd's landlord for the barber shop?

52. What is the full name of the diner?

53. Where do Andy and Barney go for Italian food?

54. Who is the organist at All Souls Church?

55. What is Aunt Bee's favorite song?

56. What was Opie's imaginary horse named?

57. Who is the Mayberry telephone operator?

58. What kind of salve did Opie and his friends try to sell?

59. Who did Charlene Darling marry?

Match the actor with the character he or she played in Mayberry, America's hometown:

1.	Andy Taylor	A.	Hal Smith
2.	Barney Fife	B.	Paul Hartman
3.	Opie	C.	George Lindsey
4.	Aunt Bea	D.	Hope Summers
5.	Helen Crump	E.	Betty Lynn
6.	Thelma Lou	F.	Andy Griffith
7.	Otis Campbell	G.	Frances Bavier
8.	Floyd Lawson	H.	Aneta Corsaut
9.	Gomer Pyle	I.	Ron Howard
10.	Goober Pyle	J.	Jack Dodson
11.	Howard Sprague	K.	Howard Morris
12.	Ernest T. Bass	L.	Howard McNear
13.	Emmett Clark	M.	Don Knotts
14.	Clara Edwards	N.	Jim Nabors

50. Andy

51. Originally, the Robinson family; later, Howard Sprague

52. The Bluebird Diner

53. Morrelli's, about halfway between Mayberry and Mt. Pilot

54. Clara Edwards

55. "Chinatown, My Chinatown"

56. Blackie

57. Sarah

58. Miracle Salve

59. Dud D. Wash

Answers to matching game:

1.	F	8.	L
2.	M	9.	N
3.	I	10.	C
4.	G	11.	J
5.	H	12.	K
6.	E	13.	B
7.	A	14.	D

M*A*S*H

If Mayberry is everybody's hometown, then the 4077th is everybody's unit. Like Andy's show, *M*A*S*H* featured good scripts acted by great actors. It was funny, and it felt like real life to us, even if we hadn't been to war or worked in an operating room. These people weren't John Waynes, but they did remind us, week in and week out, of what our fighting men and women have done for all of us, time after time.

1.   Complete this quote, "Rule number one is that young men die; and rule number two is doctors can't . . . ."

2.   What member of the 4077th has a mother who is a kleptomaniac?

3.   Where did Charles go to medical school?

4.   Do you remember the name of Colonel Potter's horse?

5.   What musical instrument did Radar play?

6.   What was Zale's first name?

7.   What convinced Hawkeye to give up drinking?

8.   What was Colonel Potter's favorite snack?

9.   Who played Radar?

10.   Who played Margaret?

TELEVISION ANSWERS

1. ". . . change rule number one."

2. Margaret

3. Harvard (where else?)

4. Sophie

5. Drums

6. Zelmo

7. His high bar tab

8. Fig Newtons dipped in Scotch

9. Gary Burghoff

10. Loretta Swit

11. What does *M*A*S*H* stand for?

12. What was Trapper's middle name?

13. Do you remember Hawkeye's hometown?

14. What was Igor's last name?

15. What nickname did B. J. give to Frank?

16. What was the name of Radar's dog?

17. In what year was Colonel Potter married?

18. What was Rizzo's first name?

19. Who died in bed with Margaret?

20. What shoe size did B. J. wear?

21. What was Radar's religion?

22. Name B. J.'s daughter.

23. What was inscribed in Margaret's wedding ring?

24. What mail order company did Radar work part-time for?

25. Which character was afraid of heights?

26. Who taught Father Mulcahy how to play poker?

27. Where was Colonel Blake's plane shot down?

28. What was the title of the last episode of M*A*S*H?

29. Name Charles's hometown.

30. Harry Morgan appeared on *M*A*S*H* before he landed the role of Colonel Potter. What other character did he play?

11. Mobile Army Surgical Hospital

12. Xavier

13. Crabapple Cove, Maine

14. Straminski

15. Ferret Face

16. Ranger

17. 1913

18. Luther

19. General "Iron Guts" Kelly

20. Size 13

21. Methodist

22. Erin

23. "Over hill, over dale, our love will *ever* fail."

24. The Style Rite Shoe Company of Storm Lake, Iowa

25. B. J.

26. The mailman

27. Over the Sea of Japan

28. "Goodbye, Farewell, Amen"

29. Boston, Massachusetts

30. Major General Bartford Hamilton Steele

31. When Radar went home, who replaced him as Company Clerk?

32. What was B. J.'s wife named?

33. What was Colonel Potter's full name?

34. How many bunks were there in the Swamp?

35. Name Margaret's husband.

36. What was Klinger's hometown?

37. Can you name the original cast?

38. Who played the part of Dr. Anthony Borelli?

39. Who was the psychiatrist?

40. What was the motto of the 4077th?

41. Who was the first person cast for *M∗A∗S∗H*?

42. How many years did *M∗A∗S∗H* run?

43. In what year was Radar born?

44. What specific neighborhood of his hometown is Charles from?

45. Who is Colonel Blake's daughter?

46. Who bragged that he had "Never given a dime to charity"?

47. What religious denomination was Major Winchester?

48. Who helps develop the chest X-rays of the nurses?

49. How old was Radar's father when he was born?

31. Corporal Klinger

32. Peg

33. Sherman T. Potter

34. Four

35. Colonel Donald Penobscott

36. Toledo, Ohio

37. Alan Alda, Wayne Rogers, McLean Stevenson,
     Loretta Swit, Larry Linville, and Gary Burghoff

38. Robert Alda (Alan's father)

39. Sidney Freedman

40. "Best Care Anywhere"

41. Gary Burghoff

42. Ten

43. 1932

44. Beacon Hill

45. Janie

46. Frank Burns

47. Presbyterian

48. Radar

49. Sixty-three

How the West Was Won

The cowboy is probably the greatest symbol of American life in the minds of foreigners and Americans alike. There's something we can't help admiring in his rugged, independent ways.

While we usually think of the cowboy life as a thing of the past, movies and television have done a great job of keeping it alive. It's the one part of our history that teachers don't have to struggle to get kids interested in. They're already interested from watching the old movies and reruns of the old TV shows. Most of them were saying "Hi-ho, Silver, away!" and "Keep them doggies movin' " as soon as they could talk.

If you still dream about riding the range and roping and bucking and branding, this is the section for you.

1. What was William S. Hart's middle name?

2. Who rode a horse named Topper?

3. What was Joel McCrea's last film?

4. What University of Alabama football hero went on to become a cowboy star?

5. Who played the sheriff in *The Man Who Shot Liberty Valance*?

6. Who rode a horse named Thunder?

7. What was Ben Johnson's first movie?

8. Who rode a horse named Ringeye?

9. Name Audie Murphy's first western film.

10. Who played Tonto on TV?

11. Who rode a horse named Buttermilk?

12. Who played the Virginian on TV?

13. Who played the Cisco Kid on TV?

14. Who played Pancho?

15. Who rode a horse named Champion?

16. Who is the only person to be in both the Cowboy Hall of Fame and the Country Music Hall of Fame?

17. Two Best Actor Oscar winners appeared in *Fort Apache*, *She Wore a Yellow Ribbon* and *Rio Grande*. One, of course, was John Wayne. Who was the other?

COWBOY ANSWERS

1. Surrey

2. Hopalong Cassidy

3. *Ride the High Country*

4. Johnny Mack Brown

5. Andy Devine

6. Red Ryder

7. *Three Godfathers*

8. Smiley Burnette

9. *The Kid from Texas*

10. Jay Silverheels

11. Dale Evans

12. James Drury

13. Duncan Renaldo

14. Leo Carrillo

15. Gene Autry

16. Tex Ritter

17. Victor McLaglen

18. Who rode a horse named Tony?

19. What was Cecil B. De Mille's first movie?

20. Who rode a horse named Rebel?

21. Who starred in the 1956 western *Jubal*?

22. Who directed *The Alamo*?

23. Who played Bronco Lane on TV?

24. Who rode a horse named White Flash?

25. Who was Red Ryder's sidekick?

26. Who was Louis Bert Lindley?

27. Who was known as the Arizona Cowboy?

28. What did Roy Rogers call his TV ranch?

29. Where did Hopalong Cassidy work?

30. What was Montgomery Cliff's first movie?

31. Who rode a horse named Razor?

32. Who starred in the 1950 movie *The Gunfighter*?

33. Who starred in the Durango Kid movies?

34. What was the name of the Durango Kid's horse?

35. What was Gabby Hayes's real first name?

36. On the Roy Rogers TV show, Dale Evans owned a cafe. Name it.

37. Name the town in *High Noon*.

18. Tom Mix

19. *The Squaw Man*

20. Johnny Mack Brown

21. Glenn Ford

22. John Wayne

23. Ty Hardin

24. Tex Ritter

25. Little Beaver

26. Slim Pickens

27. Rex Allen

28. The Double-R-Bar

29. On the Bar-20 Ranch

30. *Red River*

31. Chuck Connors in *The Rifleman*

32. Gregory Peck

33. Charles Starrett

34. Raider

35. George

36. The Eureka Cafe

37. Hadleyville

38. In 1963, Frank Sinatra and the Three Stooges appeared in a western movie together. Can you name it?

39. Who was Will Kane?

40. What was the name of the saloon on *The Rifleman*?

41. Name Sky King's ranch.

42. Name John Wayne's ranch in *Red River*.

43. Do you remember the name of the ranch in the classic western *Duel in the Sun*?

44. Where did Paladin go to college?

45. Who owned the livery stable on *Gunsmoke*?

46. Who rode a horse named Coco?

38. *Four for Texas*

39. Gary Cooper's character in *High Noon*

40. The Silver Dollar

41. The Flying Crown

42. The Red River D

43. The Spanish Bit

44. West Point

45. Moss Grimmick

46. Rex Allen

John Wayne

John Wayne made 152 motion pictures between 1928 and 1976. The official records show that he died on June 12, 1979. Fans of "The Duke" know that this is not true. We know that he will be alive as long as there is one person around who remembers Sergeant John M. Stryker, U.S.M.C., or one who remembers Rooster Cogburn with his horse's reins in his mouth, Colt in one hand, Winchester in the other, riding full tilt toward the evil and deadly Ned Pepper.

In *Time* magazine (August 8, 1969), John Wayne was quoted as saying he would like to be remembered by these words, *"Feo, Fuerte Y Formal."* The English translation: "He was ugly, was strong and had dignity."

John Wayne dead? That'll be the day.

1. What was his real name?

2. Where was he born?

3. Where did he go to college?

4. Can you name his first movie?

5. In 1949, he was nominated for the Best Actor Academy Award. Can you name the movie?

6. In 1970, he won the Oscar. Name the movie.

7. What was his first lead role?

8. What was his last movie?

9. Can you name two pictures in which John Wayne and Claire Trevor costarred?

10. Who was John Wayne's female costar in *Hondo*?

11. What was Hondo's last name?

12. Can you name Hondo's somewhat surly dog?

13. What was the name of the Apache chief in *Hondo*?

14. What actor played the pilot in *The High and the Mighty*?

15. In what movie did the Duke play a German sea captain?

16. Can you name two films that costarred John Wayne and Lauren Bacall?

17. Who was Ethan Edwards?

18. Name the evil Indian chief in *The Searchers*.

1. Marion Michael Morrison

2. Winterset, Iowa, on May 26, 1907

3. He went to the University of Southern California for two years.

4. *Mother Machree* in 1928

5. *Sands of Iwo Jima*

6. *True Grit* (1969)

7. *The Big Trail* in 1930

8. *The Shootist* (1976)

9. *Stagecoach* (1939) and *The High and the Mighty* (1954)

10. Geraldine Page

11. Lane

12. Sam

13. Vittorio

14. Robert Stack (Wayne was the copilot)

15. *The Sea Chase* (1955)

16. *Blood Alley* (1955) and *The Shootist* (1976)

17. John Wayne's character in *The Searchers* (1956)

18. Chief Scar

19. In *The Searchers*, how long did John Wayne search for his niece, Debbie?

20. Who was Joe January?

21. Can you name the only movie that the Duke appeared in with George Gobel?

22. Who was Link Appleyard?

23. In what town was *The Man Who Shot Liberty Valance* set?

24. Who was the editor of *The Shinbone Star*?

25. What did John Wayne and Lee Marvin have in common in *Donovan's Reef*?

26. What was *Donovan's Reef*?

27. What four actors played *The Sons of Katie Elder*?

28. Who played the part of Katie Elder?

29. What were the names of John Wayne's production companies?

30. What was John Wayne's rank in *The Green Berets*?

31. What was David Janssen's rank in *The Green Berets*?

32. Who directed *The Green Berets*?

33. Who was Mattie Ross?

34. What was Rooster Cogburn's real first name?

35. In *True Grit*, who played the evil Ned Pepper?

36. Who was Kirby Yorke?

19.   Five years

20.   Wayne's character in *Legend of the Lost* (1957)

21.   He made a cameo appearance in *I Married a Woman* (1958)

22.   Andy Devine's character in *The Man Who Shot Liberty Valance* (1962)

23.   Shinbone

24.   Dutton Peabody, beautifully played by Edmond O'Brien

25.   The same birthday

26.   The name of John Wayne's saloon

27.   John Wayne, Dean Martin, Earl Holliman and Michael Anderson

28.   No one—she was never seen

29.   Wayne-Fellows Productions and Batjac

30.   Colonel

31.   None—he played a civilian

32.   John Wayne

33.   Kim Darby's character in *True Grit*

34.   Reubin

35.   Robert Duvall

36.   Wayne's character in *Rio Grande*

37. Who played Wayne's son in *Rio Grande*?

38. Name the other island the marines captured in *Sands of Iwo Jima*.

39. Who played John Wayne's buddy in *The Fighting Kentuckian*?

40. Name the actors who played the godfathers in the *Three Godfathers*.

41. Who was Thomas Dunson?

42. In what movie did John Wayne play that disgusting, cigar-puffing, unshaven old drunk General William T. Sherman?

43. Who was Rance Stoddard?

44. What John Wayne movie takes its title from a hit song?

45. Name the John Wayne movie that costarred James Arness.

46. John Wayne appeared in 152 motion pictures. Can you name the ones in which his character died?

47. Most of John Wayne's films were highly profitable. However, in 1960, he produced, directed and starred in a movie that lost so much money the Duke was on the edge of bankruptcy. He had pledged his personal fortune to cover the twelve-million-dollar cost of this bomb. Can you name the movie?

48. Can you name John Wayne's wives?

49. In *Donovan's Reef*, Wayne played Donovan. What was his nickname?

50. Wayne appeared in two films with Red Buttons. Can you name them?

37. Claude Jarman, Jr.

38. Tarawa

39. Oliver Hardy

40. John Wayne, Pedro Armandariz, Harry Carey, Jr.

41. John Wayne's character in *Red River*

42. *How the West Was Won*

43. James Stewart in *The Man Who Shot Liberty Valance*

44. *North to Alaska*

45. *Big Jim McLain*

46. *Reap the Wild Wind* (1942), *The Fighting Seabees* (1944), *Wake of the Red Witch* (1949), *The Alamo* (1960), *The Man Who Shot Liberty Valance* (1962), *The Cowboys* (1972), *The Shootist* (1976)

47. *The Alamo*

48. Josephine Saenz, Esperanza Bauer, Pilar Pallete

49. Guns

50. *Hatari* (1962) and *The Longest Day* (1963)

THE FILMS OF JOHN WAYNE
1928 — *Mother Machree*
Hangman's House
1929 — *Salute*
Words and Music
1930 — *Men Without Women*
Rough Romance
Cheer Up and Smile
The Big Trail
1931 — *Girls Demand Excitement*
Three Girls Lost
Men Are Like That
Range Feud
Maker of Men
1932 — *Shadow of the Eagle*
The Hurricane Express
Haunted Gold
Texas Cyclone
Lady and Gent
Two-Fisted Law
Ride Him, Cowboy
The Big Stampede
1933 — *The Telegraph Trail*
His Private Secretary
Central Airport
Somewhere in Sonora
The Life of Jimmy Dolan
Baby Face
The Man from Monterey
Riders of Destiny
Sagebrush Trail
The Three Musketeers
1934 — *West of the Divide*
The Lucky Texan
Blue Steel
The Man from Utah
Randy Rides Alone
The Star Packer
The Trail Beyond
'Neath Arizona Skies
The Lawless Frontier

1942 — *Lady for a Night*
Reap the Wild Wind
The Spoilers
In Old California
Flying Tigers
Reunion in France
Pittsburgh
1943 — *A Lady Takes a Chance*
War of the Wildcats
1944 — *The Fighting Seabees*
Tail in the Saddle
1945 — *Flame of the Barbary Coast*
Back to Bataan
Dakota
They Were Expendable
1946 — *Without Reservations*
1947 — *Angel and the Badman*
Tycoon
1948 — *Fort Apache*
Red River
1949 — *Three Godfathers*
Wake of the Red Witch
She Wore a Yellow Ribbon
The Fighting Kentuckian
Sands of Iwo Jima
1950 — *Rio Grande*
1951 — *Operation Pacific*
Flying Leathernecks
1952 — *The Quiet Man*
Big Jim McLain
1953 — *Trouble Along the Way*
Island in the Sky
Hondo
1954 — *The High and the Mighty*
1955 — *The Sea Chase*
Blood Alley
1956 — *The Conqueror*
The Searchers

1935 — *Texas Terror*
Rainbow Valley
Paradise Canyon
The Dawn Rider
The Desert Trail
Westward Ho
The New Frontier
The Lawless Range
1936 — *The Lawless Nineties*
King of the Pecos
The Oregon Trail
Winds of the Wasteland
The Sea Spoilers
The Lonely Trail
Conflict
1937 — *California Straight Ahead*
I Cover the War
Idol of the Crowds
Adventure's End
Born to the West
1938 — *Pals of the Saddle*
Overland Stage Raiders
Santa Fe Stampede
Red River Range
1939 — *Stagecoach*
The Night Riders
Three Texas Steers
Wyoming Outlaw
New Frontier
Allegheny Uprising
1940 — *The Dark Command*
Three Faces West
The Long Voyage Home
Seven Spinners
1941 — *A Man Betrayed*
Lady from Louisiana
The Shepherd of the Hills

1957 — *The Wings of Eagles*
     Jet Pilot
     Legend of the Lost
1958 — *I Married a Woman*
     The Barbarian and the Geisha
1959 — *Rio Bravo*
     The Horse Soldiers
1960 — *The Alamo*
     North to Alaska
1961 — *The Comancheros*
1962 — *The Man Who Shot Liberty Valance*
     Hatari
     The Longest Day
     How the West Was Won
1963 — *Donovan's Reef*
     McLintock!
1964 — *Circus World*
1965 — *The Greatest Story Ever Told*
     In Harm's Way
     The Sons of Katie Elder
1966 — *Cast a Giant Shadow*
1967 — *The War Wagon*
     El Dorado
1968 — *The Green Berets*
1969 — *Hellfighters*
     True Grit
     The Undefeated
1970 — *Chisum*
     Rio Lobo
1971 — *Big Jake*
1972 — *The Cowboys*
1973 — *The Train Robbers*
     Cahill, U.S. Marshal
1974 — *McQ*
1975 — *Branigan*
     Rooster Cogburn
1976 — *The Shootist*

Let's Go To The Movies

There's nothing quite like the excitement of the moment when the lights go down and the screen comes to life in front of you in a movie theater. Actually, it's even larger than life—that's part of the magic. Television shrinks life to fit inside our dens. The movies blow it up to fit our imaginations.

Throw in a tub of popcorn, a big Co-Cola and a box of Milk Duds. Put the Duke or Marilyn Monroe or Bogie and Bacall up there twelve feet high. Sit back and enjoy. Who could ask for more?

Academy Awards

1. Name the first picture to win an Academy Award.

2. Only once have three actors been nominated for Best Actor from the same picture. Name all three actors and the picture.

3. Spencer Tracy won back-to-back oscars in 1937 and 1938. Can you name the two movies?

4. Who was the first black Oscar winner?

5. Who was the second?

6. Gary Cooper won two Best Actor Oscars. Can you name the two films?

7. Thomas Mitchell played Scarlett O'Hara's father in 1939. That same year, he won the Best Supporting Actor Oscar. Can you name the movie?

8. Can you name the only western ever to win the Best Picture award?

9. Who won the very first Best Supporting Actor award ever given?

10. For what movie did Lee Marvin win the 1965 Best Actor Award?

11. Bonnie and Clyde made a lot of money but earned only one acting award. Do you remember who won it?

1. *Wings* (1927/28)

2. The picture was *Mutiny on the Bounty* (1935). The actors were Clark Gable, Charles Laughton and Franchot Tone. (None of them won.)

3. *Captains Courageous* (1937) and *Boys Town* (1938)

4. Hattie McDaniel, for *Gone with the Wind* (1939)

5. Sidney Poitier, for *Lilies of the Field* (1963)

6. *Sergeant York* (1941) and *High Noon* (1952)

7. *Stagecoach*

8. *Cimarron* (1930/31)

9. Walter Brennan for *Come and Get It* (1936)

10. *Cat Ballou*

11. Estelle Parsons, for Best Supporting Actress (1967)

12. For what movie did Rod Steiger win his Best Actor award?

13. Who was the only father-son combo to win Oscars for the same movie?

14. Jane Wyman won her Oscar in 1948 without saying a word. Name the movie.

15. Do you remember the name of the movie that won funnyman Red Buttons his Oscar?

16. In 1945, both Bing Crosby and Barry Fitzgerald won Oscars playing priests. Name the movie.

17. Do you remember the movie for which Ben Johnson won his Oscar?

18. Name the movie for which George Burns won his Oscar.

19. Keith Carradine has never won an Oscar for his acting, but he did write the words and music for the 1975 Oscar-winning song. Name it.

20. Bob Hope's theme song was a 1938 Oscar winner. Can you name it?

21. Can you name the actor who won an Oscar playing Santa Claus?

22. Folk singer Burl Ives won the Best Supporting Actor award in 1958. Can you name the film?

23. Who was the first person to win the Best Supporting Actress Oscar?

24. Can you name the 1979 film that won Sally Field her first Best Actress Oscar?

25. Henry Fonda won the Best Actor Award for his last film. Can you name it?

12. *In the Heat of the Night* (1967)

13. Walter Huston won Best Supporting Actor and his son John won Best Director for *Treasure of Sierra Madre.*

14. *Johnny Belinda* (she played a deaf mute)

15. *Sayonara* (1957)

16. *Going My Way*

17. *The Last Picture Show* (1971)

18. *The Sunshine Boys* (1975)

19. "I'm Easy," from the movie *Nashville*

20. "Thanks for the Memory," from the *Big Broadcast of 1938*

21. Edmund Gwenn in *The Miracle on 34th Street* (1947)

22. *The Big Country*

23. Gale Sondergaard in 1936 (for *Anthony Adverse*)

24. *Norma Rae* (she also won in 1984 for *Places in the Heart*)

25. *On Golden Pond* (1981)

ACADEMY AWARDS—BEST PICTURE

1927/28 —*Wings*
1928/29 —*Broadway Melody*
1929/30 —*All Quiet on the Western Front*
1930/31 —*Cimarron*
1931/32 —*Grand Hotel*
1932/33 —*Cavalcade*
1934 —*It Happened One Night*
1935 —*Mutiny on the Bounty*
1936 —*The Great Ziegfeld*
1937 —*The Life of Émile Zola*
1938 —*You Can't Take It with You*
1939 —*Gone with the Wind*
1940 —*Rebecca*
1941 —*How Green Was My Valley*
1942 —*Mrs. Miniver*
1943 —*Casablanca*
1944 —*Going My Way*
1945 —*The Lost Weekend*
1946 —*The Best Years of Our Lives*
1947 —*Gentleman's Agreement*
1948 —*Hamlet*
1949 —*All the King's Men*
1950 —*All About Eve*
1951 —*An American in Paris*
1952 —*The Greatest Show on Earth*
1953 —*From Here to Eternity*
1954 —*On the Waterfront*
1955 —*Marty*
1956 —*Around the World in 80 Days*
1957 —*The Bridge on the River Kwai*
1958 —*Gigi*
1959 —*Ben-Hur*
1960 —*The Apartment*
1961 —*West Side Story*
1962 —*Lawrence of Arabia*
1963 —*Tom Jones*

MOVIES

1964 —*My Fair Lady*
1965 —*The Sound of Music*
1966 —*A Man for All Seasons*
1967 —*In the Heat of the Night*
1968 —*Oliver*
1969 —*Midnight Cowboy*
1970 —*Patton*
1971 —*The French Connection*
1972 —*The Godfather*
1973 —*The Sting*
1974 —*The Godfather, Part II*
1975 —*One Flew over the Cuckoo's Nest*
1976 —*Rocky*
1977 —*Annie Hall*
1978 —*The Deer Hunter*
1979 —*Kramer vs. Kramer*
1980 —*Ordinary People*
1981 —*Chariots of Fire*
1982 —*Gandhi*
1983 —*Terms of Endearment*
1984 —*Amadeus*
1985 —*Out of Africa*
1986 —*Platoon*
1987 —*The Last Emperor*

Movie Stars

They say that writers and directors and producers have a lot to do with the movies. Cameramen and make-up artists, film editors and sound engineers. I guess they do. But all I see is the stars. They're the ones that make the movies for me and for most people, I'll bet. The brighter they shine, the more we forget all the rest. Take a look at some of their faces and tease your brain with the ups and downs of the star-studded life.

Name the first Bogart and Bacall movie.

To Have and Have Not

Who is the gentleman in the picture with Mae West and Cary Grant?

1. Who played Judge Hardy in the Andy Hardy movies?

2. Who were the two lead actors in *Jesse James*?

3. Who played the title role in the 1931 version of *A Connecticut Yankee*?

4. What do cowboy star Buck Jones and funnyman Red Skelton have in common?

5. Where was Oliver Hardy born?

6. Can you name Clark Gable's first movie?

7. *Blood and Sand* has been made twice. Can you name the two actors who starred?

8. What was Cecil B. de Mille's middle name?

9. James Dean made three movies. Name them.

10. How tall was Gary Cooper?

11. Who played Amber in *Forever Amber*?

12. Who starred in the 1923 version of *The Hunchback of Notre Dame*?

13. Mercedes McCambridge won an Oscar for her first movie. Can you name the film?

14. What character did John Carradine play in *The Grapes of Wrath*?

15. Who played Dr. Frankenstein in the 1931 horror film *Frankenstein*?

16. Who said "Children of the night . . . what music they make"?

1. Lewis Stone

2. Tyrone Power and Henry Fonda

3. Will Rogers

4. Both are from Vincennes, Indiana.

5. Atlanta, Georgia (January 1892)

6. *The Painted Desert* (1930)

7. Rudolph Valentino (1922) and Tyrone Power (1941)

8. Blount

9. *East of Eden, Rebel Without a Cause* and *Giant*

10. Six feet, two inches

11. Linda Darnell

12. Lon Chaney

13. *All the King's Men*

14. Casey

15. Colin Clive

16. Bela Lugosi in *Dracula*

Name the soggy young lady in this picture.

Name the Marx Brother on the right.

Zeppo

Abbott, Costello and Laughton—can you name this
very funny film?

Abbott and Costello Meet Captain Kidd

17. Who played Mr. Chips's wife in *Goodbye Mr. Chips?*

18. Who played Carl the waiter in *Casablanca?*

19. Who starred as Pa Kettle?

20. Who starred as Ma Kettle?

21. Who starred as the oldest Kettle child?

22. Who played the priest in *San Francisco?*

23. Who was Jeanette MacDonald's real-life husband?

24. What screen beauty made her debut being chased by Groucho Marx in *Love Happy?*

25. Who played the title role in *Ruggles of Red Gap?*

26. Who was the funnyman star of David Copperfield?

27. What was Jean Harlow's last film?

28. Who played the title role in *Goodbye Mr. Chips?*

29. Who played the title role in the original *Heidi?*

30. Who played Topper in the movies?

31. Name the film that all three Barrymores (John, Ethel and Lionel) appeared in together.

32. Who killed John Wayne in *The Cowboys?*

33. Jack Nicholson and Marlon Brando costarred in a western. Can you name it?

34. Who wrote the book that *All the King's Men* was based on?

17. Greer Garson

18. S. Z. (Cuddles) Sakall

19. Percy Kilbride

20. Marjorie Main

21. Richard Long

22. Spencer Tracy

23. Gene Raymond

24. Marilyn Monroe

25. Charles Laughton

26. W. C. Fields

27. *Saratoga* (1937)

28. Robert Donat

29. Shirley Temple

30. Roland Young

31. *Rasputin*

32. Bruce Dern

33. *Missouri Breaks*

34. Robert Penn Warren

Name the young ladies with Bing.

The dog's name is Asta. Who are his two friends?

Nick and Nora Charles (Mr. and Mrs. Thin Man)

35. What was Slim Summerville's first name?

36. Jane Darwell won her Oscar for a 1940 film. Name it.

37. Can you name the three movies in which Boris Karloff appeared as the monster?

38. Who wrote *Dracula*?

39. Can you name Sonja Henie's first film?

40. Lauren Bacall met Bogart when they costarred in what film?

41. Who played the inventor of the telephone, and what was the name of the movie?

42. Who played film's first Robin Hood?

43. Who played *The Virginian* for the first time in the movies?

44. Who played the title roles in *Min and Bill*?

45. What vaudeville juggler went on to become a world-famous movie funnyman?

46. Can you name the three stars of *The Misfits*?

47. Who wrote the book *It Took Nine Tailors*?

48. What former singer starred in *Murder, My Sweet*?

49. Who starred in *Prince of Foxes*?

50. Who played the young lovers in the 1937 version of *Hurricane*?

51. In *Sunset Boulevard*, who played William Holden's girlfriend?

35. George

36. *The Grapes of Wrath*

37. *Frankenstein* (1931), *Bride of Frankenstein* (1935) and *Son of Frankenstein* (1939)

38. Bran Stoker

39. *One in a Million*

40. *To Have and Have Not*

41. Don Ameche in *The Story of Alexander Graham Bell*

42. Douglas Fairbanks (1922)

43. Dustin Farnum (1923)

44. Marie Dressler and Wallace Berry

45. W. C. Fields

46. Clark Gable, Marilyn Monroe and Montgomery Clift

47. Actor Adolphe Menjou

48. Dick Powell

49. Tyrone Power

50. Jon Hall and Dorothy Lamour

51. Nancy Olson

Name this blonde beauty.

Marie (*My Friend Irma*) Wilson

The movie was *The Yearling*. Name the deer.

Name the beauty hanging onto Mickey Rooney.

Marilyn Maxwell

This young lady was featured in *This Is Your Life*.
Who was she?

Lillian Roth

Name the bald actor shown here with Bogart.

Lee J. Cobb

Who is this man's best friend?

Harvey

Name the actor dressing Myrna Loy.

The little girl in this picture later wrote a best-selling book about the big girl in the picture. Name the book.

Mommie Dearest

Name the man sleeping on Ida Lupino's shoulder.

Alan Hale, Sr.

This Paramount picture produced the Oscar-winning song. Name the song, the picture and the two stars.

"Buttons and Bows"; *Paleface*; Bob Hope and Jane Russell

Can you name the movie that starred this very young
James Stewart?

Destry Rides Again

What was Clark Gable's character's name in *San Francisco*?

368

Blackie Norton

Name this future screen beauty.

Liz Taylor

This young lady is married to Howard Duff. Name her.

Ida Lupino

Who played the groom in *The Father of the Bride*?

Don Taylor

The beautiful lady in the middle is Ann Blythe. Can
you name her famous brother-in-law?

Dennis Day

Can you name this beautiful ex-wife of William
Holden.

24. Brenda Marshall

Gone With
The Wind

In my opinion, *Gone with the Wind* is, by far, the best
motion picture ever made. There have been countless trivia
books that deal solely with this movie. When I came up
with the following questions, I decided to stick with
questions concerning the cast of the movie. Let's see how
well you remember the wonderful folks that brought
Margaret Mitchell's masterpiece to life on the screen.

What was Rhett's hometown?

Charleston, South Carolina

Name the wimp in the middle.

Ashley Wilkes

1. Who played the part of the evil, no-account Jonas Wilkerson?

2. Who played Big Sam?

3. Who played Mammy?

4. Who played Suellen O'Hara?

5. Who played Carreen O'Hara?

6. Who played Prissy?

7. Who played Bonnie Blue Butler?

8. Who played Aunt Pittypat?

9. Who played Uncle Peter?

10. Who played Tom, the Yankee captain?

11. Who played Charles Hamilton?

12. Who played the Yankee deserter that Scarlett killed?

13. Who played Belle Watling?

14. Who played Dr. Meade?

15. Who played Mrs. Merriwether?

16. Who played Frank Kennedy?

17. Which member of the cast went on to become Clark Kent?

18. Can you name Thomas Mitchell's TV series?

19. Which member of the *Gone with the Wind* cast was also a sidekick to Hopalong Cassidy?

1. Victor Jory

2. Everett Brown

3. Hattie McDaniel

4. Evelyn Keyes

5. Ann Rutherford

6. Butterfly McQueen

7. Cammie King

8. Laura Hope Crews

9. Eddie Anderson

10. Ward Bond

11. Rand Brooks

12. Paul Hurst

13. Ona Munson

14. Harry Davenport

15. Jane Darwell

16. Carroll Nye

17. George Reeves, who played Stuart Tarleton

18. *O'Henry's Playhouse*

19. Rand Brooks

20. What was Vivian Leigh's salary for *Gone with the Wind*?

21. How many actresses were interviewed for the part of Scarlett?

22. How did Leslie Howard die?

23. Which two cast members took their own lives?

24. How old was Leslie Howard when he appeared as Ashley?

25. What cast member also played Polly Benedict in the Andy Hardy films?

20. She made thirty thousand dollars for 125 shooting days

21. Fourteen hundred

22. He was on an airliner that was shot down by German fighters. It was said that the German high command thought Winston Churchill was on board.

23. Ona Munson (Belle Watling) and George Reeves (Stuart Tarleton)

24. Forty-Five

25. Ann Rutherford

See You in the Funny Papers

When you were a kid, what was the first part of the newspaper you wanted to get your hands on? The funny papers, right? The comics. It may be the first thing anybody ever read to you, the first thing you actually wanted to read for yourself. Some people may tell you they turn to the international news or the editorial page first. But I'm willing to admit it—I still go for the funnies. Besides, don't they have some cartoons on that editorial page, anyhow? Indulge yourself in trivia's funniest facts. Be a kid again.

1. Who was Flash Gordon's girlfriend?

2. Who was Skeezix Wallet?

3. Who wrote Dick Tracy?

4. Who was Andy and Min Gump's son?

5. What do *B.C.* and *The Wizard of Id* have in common?

6. Who created *Red Ryder*?

7. Name the comic strip whose hero is a baldheaded little boy who never spoke.

8. What do *Hi and Lois* and *Beetle Bailey* have in common?

9. Who was Knobby Walsh?

10. Who created *Dennis the Menace*?

11. Name a comic strip that was set entirely in Canada.

12. Who was Snuffy Smith's best friend?

13. How old was Li'l Abner?

14. How tall was Li'l Abner?

15. What was Mammy Yokum's first name?

16. What was Pappy Yokum's full name?

17. What was Little Annie Rooney's dog named?

18. How old was Little Annie Rooney?

1. Dale Arden

2. One of the *Gasoline Alley* characters

3. Chester Gould

4. Chester Gump

5. Both are drawn by Johnny Hart.

6. Fred Harman

7. Henry

8. Both are the brainchild of Mort Walker.

9. Joe Palooka's fight manager

10. Hank Ketcham

11. *King of the Royal Mounted*

12. Barney Google

13. Nineteen

14. 6'3"

15. Pansy

16. Lucifer Ornamental Yokum

17. Zero

18. Twelve

19. Name Little Orphan Annie's dog.

20. Who was the giant sidekick of Mandrake the Magician?

21. Can you name Mark Trail's Dog?

22. What color hair did Little Orphan Annie have?

23. What was the original name of the comic strip *Mary Worth*?

24. Who created the comic strip *Brenda Starr*?

25. Who is Brenda Starr's love interest?

26. Can you name Moon Mullins's little brother?

27. What was Moon Mullins's real first name?

28. What was Smilin' Jack's last name?

29. Who was Smilin' Jack's wife?

30. What was the very first continually published six-day-a-week comic strip?

31. Who created *Mutt and Jeff*?

32. Name Nancy's boyfriend.

33. Name Dagwood's daughter.

34. Name Blondie's son.

35. Can you name Blondie and Dagwood's dog?

36. Financially, what is the most successful comic strip of all time?

19. Sandy

20. Lothar

21. Andy

22. Red

23. *Apple Annie*

24. Dale Messick

25. The mystery man Basil St. John

26. Kayo

27. Moonshine

28. Martin

29. Joy

30. *Mutt and Jeff*

31. Bud Fisher

32. Sluggo

33. Cookie

34. Alexander

35. Daisy

36. *Peanuts.* It is estimated that the strip and strip-related ventures bring in more than fifty million dollars a year.

37. What was the original name of the *Peanuts* comic strip?

38. What is Pigpen's last name?

39. Who was known as "The Ghost Who Walks"?

40. Who was the Phantom's girlfriend?

41. What famous comic strip was set in the Okefenokee Swamp?

42. Who is Rex Morgan's nurse?

43. Can you name the comic strip created by famed writer Dashiell Hammett?

44. What comic-strip hero played both pro baseball and pro football?

45. What was the original name of the comic strip *Smilin' Jack*?

46. Do you remember the comic strip about a zany fireman?

47. What comic strip was based on a cowboy movie series?

48. In *Terry and the Pirates*, who was Terry's best friend?

49. What was Tillie the Toiler's last name?

50. Who was Tillie the Toiler's boyfriend?

51. Who was Tim Tyler's sidekick?

37. *Li'l Folks*

38. Franklin

39. The Phantom

40. Diana Palmer

41. *Pogo*

42. June Gale

43. *Secret Agent X-9*

44. Ozark Ike

45. *On the Wing*

46. *Smokey Stover*

47. Hopalong Cassidy

48. Pat Ryan

49. Jones

50. Mac

51. Spud Slavins

Turn Your Radios On

Long before there was television, Americans gathered around their radios and listened to dramas, comedies, music and more. Radio made the world bigger, and although much has changed in radio, like everything else, many of us still remember those good old days with fondness. These questions may create a generation gap among players, but if you remember radio's golden days, you'll be on the right side of that gap.

1. Can you name the young comic who was Jack Benny's summer replacement in 1947 and went on to become a TV superstar?

2. How did columnist Walter Winchell begin his Sunday broadcasts?

3. What was Young Widder Brown's first name?

4. Who was the host of *The Kraft Music Hall* from 1935 to 1946?

5. Can you name four actors who played the Shadow?

6. What was Just Plain Bill's last name?

7. Who was Jimmy Durante's radio partner from 1943 through 1946?

8. What was Fibber McGee and Molly's address?

9. What was Just Plain Bill's occupation?

10. Who played Irma on *My Friend Irma*?

11. Who played Duffy on *Duffy's Tavern*?

12. In what town did Just Plain Bill work?

13. What was Irma's last name on *My Friend Irma*?

14. What did Jimmy Durante say at the end of his weekly program?

15. Where was Our Gal Sunday born?

16. Who was Sunday's husband?

17. How did the lead-in identify Sunday's husband?

1. Jack Paar

2. "Good evening, Mr. and Mrs. North and South
   America and all the ships at sea. Let's go to press."

3. Ellen

4. Bing Crosby

5. Robert Hardy Andrews, Orson Welles, Bill Johnstone
   and Bret Morrison

6. Davidson

7. Garry Moore

8. 79 Wistful Vista

9. Barber

10. Marie Wilson

11. Nobody. He was never seen. Ed Gardner played
    Archie, the manager.

12. Hartville

13. Peterson

14. "Good night, Mrs. Calabash, wherever you are."
    That was his pet name for his first wife, Jeanne,
    who died in 1943.

15. Silver Creek, Colorado

16. Lord Henry Brinthrope

17. As a "wealthy and titled Englishman"

18. What did Digger O'Dell do for a living?

19. Who was the host of *The Fleischmann Hour*?

20. Who played Daisy June, Calamity Jane and Mrs. Willy Lump-Lump on the *Red Skelton Show*?

21. The *First-Nighter Program* was aired from what mythical theater?

22. What was Helen Trent's occupation?

23. Portia Blake faced life everyday. What was her occupation?

24. To whom was Portia married?

25. What TV game-show host played Superman on radio?

26. What famous radio show was sponsored by the Pacific Coast Borax Company?

27. What actor was the first to play Steve Wilson on *Big Town*?

28. On what radio program was the classic "Wrong Number" first heard, and who starred in it?

29. What husband/wife team produced more soap operas than any other persons in radio history?

30. Who was famous for saying "Coming, Mother"?

31. What quiz show had "The Secret Word"?

32. What did Red Ryder say when he wanted his horse to go fast?

18. Undertaker on *The Life of Riley*

19. Rudy Vallee

20. Harriet Hilliard (Mrs. Ozzie Nelson)

21. The Little Theatre Off Times Square

22. Dress designer

23. Attorney

24. Walter Manning

25. Clayton "Bud" Collyer

26. *Death Valley Days*

27. Edward G. Robinson

28. *Suspense*, starring Agnes Moorehead

29. Frank and Anne Hummert

30. Henry Aldrich

31. *You Bet Your Life*

32. "Roll, Thunder, Roll"

33. What did Mandrake's utterance *"Invoco legem magiciarium"* mean?

34. What product sponsored *Ma Perkins*?

35. What was Ma Perkins's occupation?

36. In what town did Ma Perkins live?

37. What was the name of Ma's faithful employee?

38. Who played Aunt Fanny on *The Breakfast Club*?

39. Who was the creator of the comic strip *Mark Trail*, on which the radio show was based?

40. What Atlanta man once played the same role as Hattie McDaniel later played in a radio comedy?

41. What was Vic and Sade's last name?

42. Which soap opera included the characters of Dottie Brainfeeble, Hank Gumpox, Cora Bucksaddle, and Botch Purney?

43. Who was the most famous narrator of *The March of Time*?

44. Who was famous for saying "What a revoltin' development this is"?

45. Who played Daddy on *The Baby Snooks Show*?

46. Who was the Colgate Shave Cream Man?

47. What young wireless operator on Nantucket Island, Massachusetts, recieved the news of the Titanic's collision with an iceberg?

33. "I invoke the law of magic."

34. Oxydol

35. She ran a lumberyard.

36. Rushville Center

37. Shuffle Shober

38. Fran Allison of *Kukla, Fran and Ollie* fame

39. Atlanta's own Ed Dodd

40. Bob Corley and Hattie McDaniel both played Beulah on the radio show named for their character. Beulah was also played by Marlin Hurt, Louise Beavers and Lillian Randolph.

41. Gook

42. *Vic and Sade*

43. Westbrook Van Voorhis

44. Chester A. Riley

45. Hanley Stafford

46. Bill Steen

47. David Sarnoff, later founder and president of RCA and NBC

48. What was the earlier name of the American Broadcasting Corporation?

49. Name Buster Brown's dog.

50. Who played the mayor in *The Mayor of the Town*?

51. Joan Davis was the central character in which soap opera?

52. Dr. Jim Brent was a featured character on which soap opera?

53. By what name did we know Billy Jones and Ernie Hare?

54. What was unusual about the appearance of broadcaster Floyd Gibbons?

55. Who was the host of *Welcome Traveler*?

56. Who said, "Heigh-ho, everybody"?

57. What was the actual relationship of the actresses who played Myrt and Marge?

58. On which soap opera were Chichi and Papa David the central characters?

59. Who was the original host of the *Original Amateur Hour*?

60. Ezra Stone and Jackie Kelk appeared on what show and in what roles?

61. Who used the comedy tag line "That's a joke, son"?

62. Who was the Arkansas Traveler?

48.   The Blue Network (part of NBC)

49.   Tige

50.   Lionel Barrymore

51.   *When a Girl Marries*

52.   *Road of Life*

53.   The Happiness Boys—they recorded the world's first commercial jingle for Interwoven socks.

54.   He wore a patch over his left eye, which he lost in WWI.

55.   Tommy Bartlett

56.   Rudy Vallee

57.   They were mother (Myrtle Vail) and daughter (Donna Dameral).

58.   *Life Can Be Beautiful*

59.   Major Edward Bowes, later followed by Jay C. Flippen and Ted Mack

60.   Henry Aldrich and Home Brown on *The Aldrich Family*

61.   Kenny Delmar as Senator Claghorn on *The Fred Allen Show*

62.   Bob Burns

63. Who was married to Lorenzo Jones?

64. Although it was technically not a soap opera, *The Johnson Family* was a serial that featured one man who played all the characters. What was his name?

65. What was the name of Lum 'n' Abner's store?

66. Willie Jefferson was a character on *Amos 'n' Andy*. He was also known by another name. What was it?

67. Who was the creator of *Meet the Press*?

68. Name Buck Rogers's archenemy.

69. In which soap opera was the minister Dr. John Rutledge the central character?

70. *Wendy Warren and the News* was introduced by one of the best-known news commentators in radio and television history. Who was he?

71. Where did the Fat Man weigh himself at the beginning of each show?

72. On the *Mickey Mouse Theater of the Air*, who was the voice of Mickey?

73. Who was Orson Welles's coproducer on the *Mercury Theatre on the Air*?

74. Who was the Dragon Lady?

75. Who was Captain Midnight's archenemy?

76. What soap opera had as its theme song "Funiculi, Funicula"?

77. While it was technically not a soap opera, it was one of the first of the daily serials. Its original title was *Sam 'n' Henry*, and it later achieved perhaps the largest percentage audience of any program ever to appear on radio or television. What was the ultimate name of this legendary show?

63. Belle

64. Jimmy Scribner

65. The Jot 'Em Down Store

66. Lightnin'

67. Martha Rountree

68. Killer Kane

69. *The Guiding Light*

70. Douglas Edwards

71. In a drugstore

72. Walt Disney

73. John Houseman

74. Archenemy of Terry Lee on *Terry and the Pirates*

75. Ivan Shark

76. *Lorenzo Jones*

77. *Amos 'n' Andy*

78. How did the Mysterious Traveler travel?

79. Who led the orchestra on the *Bell Telephone Hour*?

80. Who knew "what evil lurks in the hearts of men"?

81. What did the Green Hornet call his car?

82. Who was the chief accountant of the Consolidated Kitchenware Company, Plant No. 14 in Crooper, Illinois?

83. Gil Whitney was the long-time lover of what soap opera character?

84. Who played Walter Denton on *Our Miss Brooks*?

85. Freeman Gosden and Charles Correll were two characters on radio in Chicago before they were Amos 'n' Andy. Who were they?

86. Who was known as the Robin Hood of Modern Crime?

87. Who was Sam Spade's secretary?

88. What was the name of the lady who lived on Honeymoon Hill?

89. The relationship between John Perry and his secretary was the theme of what soap opera?

90. What was the name of the telephone operator on *Fibber McGee and Molly*?

78. By train

79. Donald Voorhees

80. The Shadow

81. Black Beauty

82. Victor Rodney Gook of *Vic and Sade*

83. Helen Trent

84. Richard Crenna

85. Sam 'n' Henry on WGN

86. The Saint

87. Effie Perrine

88. Amanda

89. *John's Other Wife*

90. Myrt

91. Who sponsored *The March of Time*?

92. Who was host of the *Lux Radio Theatre*?

93. Who was known as the Texaco Fire Chief?

94. What was Young Doctor Malone's first name?

95. Several memorable songs served as themes for various soap operas. Name the soap operas which had the following songs as themes:

   a. "Poor Butterfly"

   b. "Red River Valley"

   c. "Estrelita"

   d. "In the Gloaming"

   e. "Believe Me, If All These Endearing Young Charms"

   f. "Claire de Lune"

96. Which soap opera was set in the town of Glen Falls?

97. Who played Hopalong Cassidy on radio?

98. What was the theme song of *The Railroad Hour*?

99. What was the first heavyweight boxing championship to be on radio?

100. Who was the first U.S. President to speak on radio?

101. What was the name of Stella Dallas's daughter?

102. On which soap opera did a husband and wife ultimately become United States Senators?

91. *Time* magazine

92. Cecil B. De Mille

93. Ed Wynn

94. Jerry

95. a. *Myrt and Marge*

    b. *Our Gal Sunday*

    c. *Valiant Lady*

    d. *Young Widder Brown*

    e. *Aunt Jenny*

    f. *The Story of Mary Marlin*

96. *Big Sister*

97. William "Bill" Boyd

98. "I've Been Working on the Railroad"

99. Jack Dempsey versus George Carpentier (7/2/21)

100. Woodrow Wilson (7/14/19); Harding was the second (6/14/22)

101. Laurel (Lolly Baby)

102. *The Story of Mary Marlin*

103. Who played the Bickersons on the *Edgar Bergen and Charlie McCarthy Show*?

104. What character on *Amos 'n' Andy* was played by the same person on both radio and television?

105. Who said "Up, up and away"?

106. What did Jimmy Fidler do on radio?

107. Who said "I dood it"?

108. What long-time radio and TV actor was the voice of Pepper Young?

109. What was Mary Noble known as?

110. What product sponsored *Little Orphan Annie* on radio?

111. Who played Jack Benny's wife on his radio program?

112. Who sponsored Tom Mix?

113. Who was known as America's Famous Fighting Cowboy?

114. Who said, "Oh, George, I'll bet you say that to all the girls"?

115. Leila Ransom was a character on a comedy show. Who was her boyfriend?

116. Who played Hopalong Cassidy's sidekick, California Carlson?

117. Who lived on Melody Ranch?

118. What soap opera family contained the characters of Molly, Jake, Rosalie and Sammy?

103. Don Ameche and Frances Langford

104. Sapphire Stevens (played by Ernestine Wade)

105. Superman

106. A show-business gossip show

107. Red Skelton as Junior, the Mean Widdle Kid

108. Mason Adams

109. Backstage Wife

110. Ovaltine (Did you get your decoder ring?)

111. His real-life wife, Mary Livingston

112. Ralston Cereals

113. Red Ryder

114. Gracie Allen, to her husband, George Burns

115. Throckmorton P. Gildersleeve of *The Great Gildersleeve*

116. Andy Clyde

117. Gene Autry

118. *The Goldbergs*

119. What soap opera had as its central locale the Slightly Read Book Shop?

120. What was the name of the mayor on *Fibber McGee and Molly*?

121. Larry Parks played Al Jolson in the movie *The Jolson Story*. In the Lux Radio Theatre version, who played Jolson?

122. Who was the sponsor of *Jack Armstrong, All-American Boy*?

123. Who sponsored *Your Hit Parade*?

124. What was David Farrell also known as?

125. Bess Johnson was the name of the central character in the soap opera *Hilltop House*. Who played Bess Johnson?

126. Who played Matt Dillon on radio's *Gunsmoke*?

127. How did Major Bowes end the acts on the *Original Amateur Hour*?

128. Which soap opera was set in the Three Oaks Medical Center?

129. What was the top dollar prize on *Take It or Leave It*?

130. Who played Sam Spade on radio?

131. What was Amos's little girl's name on *Amos 'n' Andy*?

132. While it was generally called a serial drama, this evening radio series had all the characteristics of a soap opera. Its author was Carleton E. Morse. What was it called?

119. *Life Can Be Beautiful*

120. Mayor La Trivia, portrayed by Gale Gordon

121. Jolson himself

122. Wheaties

123. Lucky Strike cigarettes

124. Front-Page Farrell

125. Bess Johnson

126. William Conrad

127. With a large gong

128. *Young Doctor Malone*

129. $64.00

130. Howard Duff

131. Arbadella

132.. *One Man's Family*

133. What does L.S./M.F.T. stand for?

134. What is the world's most honored watch?

135. Who played the title role in *Pat Novak for Hire*?

136. Who was "Enemy to those who make him an enemy, friend to those who have no friends"?

137. This talented writer and his wife built an early radio soap opera around the wife's malaprops. Who were they, and what was the name of the show?

138. *The Brighter Day, The Guiding Light, Against the Storm* and *Search for Tommorrow* were radio soap operas which had something in common. What was it?

139. Who played Jim Anderson on *Father Knows Best* on radio?

140. What well-known Atlanta broadcaster was once a writer for the radio program *The FBI in Peace and War*?

141. What did Doctor I.Q. give away?

142. Some soap operas had more than one name. A well-known soap opera was called *Red Adams, Red Davis* and *Forever Young* before it finally became known under its long-time title in 1936. Which show was it?

143. What well-known soap opera opened to the strains of "How Can I Leave Thee?"

144. Who was Lily Ruskin?

133. Lucky Strike Means Fine Tobacco (Remember when Lucky Strike Green went to war?)

134. Longines

135. Jack Webb

136. Boston Blackie

137. Goodman and Jane Ace of *Easy Aces*

138. They later became television soap operas.

139. Robert Young, who also played the role on TV

140. Elmo Ellis of WSB radio

141. Silver dollars

142. *Pepper Young's Family*

143. *Stella Dallas*

144. Spring Byington's character in *December Bride*, which went from radio to TV

145. On what soap opera was the audience advised to "Keep thy head bowed, for the greatest storm the world has ever known came to an end one sunny morning"?

146. General Mills sponsored many soap operas. Who was the spokesperson for General Mills's Products?

147. What radio newscaster was heard daily from 6:45 to 7:00 P.M. EST for fifty years?

145. *Against the Storm*

146. Betty Crocker

147. Lowell Thomas

When Bands Were Big
and Music Was Music

I don't know exactly what happened, but it did. They starting calling noise music and forgot how music really sounds. It has instruments you recognize played by virtuoso performers. It has words that singers sing in voices that you want to listen to. The words make sense.

Call me old-fashioned, but I like the big-band sound—the singers, the songs, the musicians. This section is another one that might create friction between generations. If that happens, just put on a Glenn Miller record and tell the ones who can't answer the questions to listen carefully.

Here are some famous nicknames. Do you know the real names of these musicians and the instrument each played?

1. Duke Ellington

2. Count Basie

3. Satchmo

4. Dizzy Gillespie

5. Cab Calloway

6. Bix Beiderbecke

7. Buddy Rich

8. Tex Beneke

9. Cootie Williams

10. Chu Berry

11. Yank Lawson

12. Hot Lips Page

13. Muggsy Spanier

14. Ziggy Elman

15. Mezz Mezzero

16. Toots Mandela

17. Stuff Smith

18. Pee Wee Hunt

19. Pee Wee Russell

1. Edward Ellington, Piano

2. William Basie, Piano

3. Louis Armstrong, Trumpet

4. John Gillespie, Trumpet

5. Cabell Calloway, Drums

6. Leon Beiderbecke, Cornet

7. Bernard Rich, Drums

8. Gordon Beneke, Sax

9. Charles Williams, Trumpet

10. Leon Berry, Trumpet

11. John Lawson, Trumpet

12. Oran Page, Trumpet

13. Francis Spanier, Trumpet

14. Harry Finkleman, Trumpet

15. Milton Mezzere, Trombone

16. Nuncie Mandela, Sax

17. Gordon Smith, Violin

18. Walter Hunt, Trombone

19. Charles Russell, Clarinet

20. Peanuts Hucke

21. Fatha Hines

22. Sweets Edison

23. Slim Gaillard

24. Slam Stewart

25. Chubby Jackson

26. Jelly Roll Morton

27. Skitch Henderson

28. Buddy Morrow

29. Zoot Sims

30. Alvino Rey

31. Blue Barron

32. Ishabibble Begue

33. Wingy Manone

34. Spike Jones

35. Shorty Sherook

36. Cannonball Adderly

37. Bird Parker

38. Rudy Vallee

20. Michael Hucke, Sax

21. Earl Hines, Piano

22. Harry Edison, Sax

23. Bulee Gaillard, Guitar

24. Leroy Stewart, Bass

25. Grieg Jackson, Piano

26. Ferdinand de Menthe, Piano

27. Lyle Henderson, Piano

28. Moe Zudecoff, Trombone

29. Jack Sims, Sax

30. Al McBurney, Guitar

31. Harry Friedland, Leader

32. Merwyn Bogue, Trumpet

33. Joseph Manone, Trumpet

34. Spike Jones, Drums

35. Clarence Sherook, Trumpet

36. Julian Adderly, Sax

37. Charlie Parker, Sax

38. Herbert Vallee, Sax

39. Artie Shaw

40. Pres Young

41. Pinetop Smith

42. Red Nichols

43. Sy Oliver

44. Dean Hudson

45. Zutty Singleton

Can you name the principal male vocalists of these big bands?

1. Tommy Dorsey

2. Harry James

3. Count Basie

4. Ted Weems

5. Paul Whiteman

6. Artie Shaw

7. Earl Hines

8. Glenn Miller

9. Jimmy Dorsey

10. Freddy Martin

39. Abraham Arshawsky, Clarinet

40. Lester Young, Sax

41. Clarence Smith, Piano

42. Ernest Nichols, Cornet

43. Melvin Oliver, Trumpet

44. Robert Brown, Leader

45. Arthur Singleton, Drums

1. Frank Sinatra, Jack Leonard

2. Frank Sinatra, Dick Haymes

3. Jimmy Rushing, Joe Williams

4. Perry Como

5. Bing Crosby

6. Tony Pastor

7. Billy Eckstein

8. Ray Eberle, Johnny Desmond

9. Bob Eberly

10. Merv Griffin

11. Kay Kyser

12. Hal Kemp

13. Andy Kirk

14. Dick Jurgens

15. Sammy Kaye

16. Wayne King

17. Ray Noble

18. Jan Savitt

19. Les Brown

20. Glen Gray

21. Guy Lombardo

22. Fred Waring

23. Ina Ray Hutton

24. Duke Ellington

25. Jimmie Lunceford

26. Horace Heidt

11. Mike Douglas, Harry Babbitt, Sully Mason

12. Skinny Ennis

13. Pha Terrell

14. Eddy Howard, Harry Cool

15. Don Vornell

16. Buddy Clark

17. Al Bowly

18. Bon Bon (George Tunnel)

19. Butch Stone

20. Kenny Sargent

21. Carmen Lombardo

22. Johnny "Scat" Davis

23. Stuart Foster

24. Al Hibbler

25. Dan Grissom

26. Gordon McCrae

Can you name the principal female vocalists of these big bands?

1. Benny Goodman

2. Jimmy Dorsey

3. Tommy Dorsey

4. Harry James

5. Charlie Barnet

6. Glenn Miller

7. Tony Pastor

8. Anson Weeks

9. Hal Kemp

10. Gene Krupa

11. Chick Webb

12. Red Norvo

13. Kay Kyser

14. Boyd Raeburn

15. Will Bradley

16. Orrin Tucker

17. Lionel Hampton

18. Earl Hines

19. Stan Kenton

1. Helen Ward, Mary Ann McCall, Peggy Lee, Louise Tobin, Martha Tilton

2. Helen O'Connell, June Richmond, Kitty Kallen

3. Edythe Wright, Connie Haines, Jo Stafford

4. Helen Forrest, Connie Haines, Kitty Kallen

5. Lena Horne, Kay Starr, Mary Ann McCall

6. Marion Hutton, Paula Kelly

7. Rosemary Clooney, Eugenia Baird

8. Dale Evans

9. Nan Wynn, Maxine Grey, Janet Blair

10. Irene Daye, Anita O'Day

11. Ella Fitzgerald

12. Mildred Bailey

13. Ginny Simms, Trudy Erwin, Georgia Carrel

14. Ginny Powell

15. Louise Tobin, Carlotta Dale

16. Bonnie Baker

17. Dinah Washington

18. Sarah Vaughn

19. Anita O'Day, June Cristy, Chris Connor, Ann Richards

20. Artie Shaw

21. Les Brown

22. Herbie Kay

23. Ozzie Nelson

24. Ted Fio Rite

25. Ted Weems

26. George Hall

27. Charlie Spivak

28. Vincent Lopez

29. Woody Herman

30. Lucky Millinder

31. Freddy Slack

32. George Olsen

33. Teddy Wilson

34. Art Jarret

35. Frankie Masters

36. Jerry Wald

37. Mitchell Ayres

38. Louis Prima

39. Jack Jenny

20. Billie Holiday, Helen Forrest

21. Betty Bonney, Doris Day

22. Dorothy Lamour

23. Harriet Hilliard

24. Betty Grable

25. Marvel (Marilyn) Maxwell

26. Dolly Dawn

27. Irene Daye

28. Betty Hutton

29. Mary Ann McCall, Frances Wayne

30. Rosetta Tharpe

31. Ella Mae Morse

32. Ethel Shutta

33. Thelma Carpenter

34. Gail Robbins

35. Marion Frances

36. Anita Boyer

37. Mary Ann Mercer

38. Keely Smith

39. Bonnie Lake

40. Duke Elllington

41. Randy Brooks

42. Jan Savitt

43. Alvino Rey

44. Teddy Powell

45. Red Nichols

46. Vaughn Monroe

47. Johnny Long

48. Dean Hudson

49. Frankie Carle

50. John Kirby

51. Jan Garber

52. Fred Waring

53. Johnny Bethwell

54. Claude Thornhill

55. Xavier Cugat

56. Beasley Smith

57. Raymond Scott

58. Glen Gray

59. Bob Chester

40. Ida James, Ivy Anderson, Joya Sherrill

41. Ina Ray Hutton

42. Gloria de Haven

43. Yvonne King

44. Peggy Mann

45. Ruth Etting

46. Marilyn Duke

47. Helen Young

48. Frances Colwell

49. Margie Hughes (Carle-daughter)

50. Maxine Sullivan

51. Liz Tilton

52. Priscilla Lane, Rosemary Lane

53. Claire ('Shanty) Hogan

54. Fran Warren

55. Lina Romay, Abbie Lane, Charo

56. Dinah Shore

57. Dorothy Collins

58. Eugenia Baird

59. Delores O'Neil

60. Bob Crosby

61. Dorsey Brothers

62. Rudy Vallee

63. Sammy Kaye

64. Hal McIntyre

65. Charlie Spivak

66. Phil Harris

67. Will Hudson

68. Andy Kirk

Can you name the theme songs of these big bands?

1.	Benny Goodman	14.	Claude Thornhill
2.	Stan Kenton	15.	Les Brown
3.	Lionel Hampton	16.	Harry James
4.	Charlie Barnet	17.	Jimmy Dorsey
5.	Gene Krupa	18.	Artie Shaw
6.	Bunny Berigan		
7.	Perez Prado		
8.	Ted Weems		
9.	Tommy Dorsey		
10.	Count Basie		
11.	Duke Ellington		
12.	Glenn Miller		
13.	Buddy Morrow		

60.	Marion Mann	65.	June Hutton, Irene Daye
61.	Kay Weber	66.	Leah Ray
62.	Alice Faye	67.	Georgia Gibbs
63.	Janet Blair	68.	June Richmond
64.	Gloria Van		

1. "Let's Dance" (Closing: "Goodbye")

2. "Artistry in Rhythm"

3. "Flying Home"

4. "Cherokee" (Original: "I Lost Another Sweetheart")

5. "Starburst" (Original: "Apruksody")

6. "I Can't Get Started with You"

7. "Cherry Pink and Apple Blossom White"

8. "Out of the Night"

9. "I'm Getting Sentimental over You"

10. "One O'Clock Jump"

11. "Take the 'A' Train" (Original: "Mood Indigo")

12. "Moonlight Serenade"

13. "Night Train"

14. "Snowfall"

15. "Leap Frog" (Original: "Sentimental Journey")

16. "Ciribiribin"

17. "Contrasts"

18. "Nightmare"

The Sporting Life

Whether you're a spectator or a participant, sports can provide some of the greatest thrills and the most impressive displays of courage and character around these days. Even if you don't like basketball, you have to admire what Kareem can do at forty and what Spud Webb can accomplish at about five and a half feet. Most of the U.S. is too warm for hockey, but rarely has the whole country been more excited than it was when our team beat the Russians in the 1980 Winter Olympics.

Whether you're an armchair quarterback or a .300-hitter, I guarantee you'll find questions here to provide trivial thrills of victory and agonies of defeat.

1. Henry Aaron, Babe Ruth and Willie Mays are major league baseball's three career leaders in home runs. They share a unique distinction relating to the beginning and end of their careers. What is it?

2. What does A.A.U. stand for?

3. When Bobby Thomson hit his dramatic pennant-winning home run off Ralph Branca in the 1951 playoff game against the Brooklyn Dodgers, who was in the on-deck circle?

4. When Mickey Mantle broke in with the New York Yankees in 1951, what was his uniform number? Why did it change later on?

5. Speaking of Mantle, the Yankee slugger holds the all-time record for the most games in which a batter homered from both the left and right sides of the plate. How many times did Mantle accomplish this feat? Who ranks second to Mantle in this switch-hitting category?

6. Where is the Grand National Steeplechase held?

7. The first grand-slam home run in a World Series was hit in 1920 by Elmer Smith of Cleveland. When was the second grand-slam hit in Series play and by whom?

8. What other unusual event occurred in the 1920 World Series, one that has never again been accomplished in a Series game?

9. Who was the first million-dollar winner in the history of the Professional Bowlers Association?

10. Who was the youngest player ever to win a Wimbledon tennis match?

11. In 1956, Don Larsen of the New York Yankees pitched the only perfect game in World Series history. Who made the final out? What was the final score? Who was the losing pitcher?

1.   Each of these sluggers began his career and ended it in the same city but with a different team: Aaron (Milwaukee Braves and Brewers); Ruth (Boston Red Sox and Braves); Mays (New York Giants and Mets).

2.   Amateur Athletic Union

3.   Willie Mays

4.   Mantle originally wore number 6. In mid-season he was sent to Kansas City for one month. When he returned, Bobby Brown (now president of the American League) had come back from the Army and reclaimed his number (6), so Mantle was given number 7.

5.   Ten; Eddie Murray of Baltimore, with eight

6.   Aintree Course, Liverpool, England

7.   Thirty-one years later when Gil McDougald of the New York Yankees hit the one against the New York Giants

8.   An unassisted triple play—by Bill Wambsgans of Cleveland

9.   Earl Anthony

10.   Tracy Austin (at fourteen)

11.   Dale Mitchell struck out. The score was 2–0. The losing pitcher was Sal Maglie.

12. What pro football player scored the most points in one game?

13. Nine players have won back-to-back Most Valuable Player awards. Ironically, the nine players make up a full team, position by position. Can you name them?

14. Who was the youngest manager to win a pennant?

15. What NFL quarterback holds the record for the fewest passes being intercepted in a season?

16. Who was the youngest player to win a batting title? Who was the oldest?

17. In Yankee Stadium there are seven monuments in center field. Only one is to a man who never played, managed, coached, owned a team or broadcast its games. Who is he?

18. Who did Joe Louis beat to become the heavyweight champ?

19. There are only two men in the Baseball Hall of Fame who never played, managed, coached, owned a team or broadcast its games. Who are they, and why are they there?

20. Between 1957 and 1987, one team produced more than one-third of its league's batting champions. Which team, and how many batting champions?

21. Who was "Mr. Inside"?

22. Who was Eddie Gaedel, and what was his number?

23. If Eddie Gaedel was the shortest player in baseball history, who was the tallest?

24. Who was known as Mr. Pro Football?

25. What player hit a home run in his very first major league at bat, played for twenty-three more years and never hit another?

12. Ernie Nevers scored six touchdowns and four PATs while a Chicago Cardinal on November 23, 1929.

13. Hal Newhouser (p) 1944-45
Yogi Berra (c) 1954-55
Jimmy Foxx (1b) 1932-33
Joe Morgan (2b) 1975-76
Mike Schmidt (3b) 1980-81
Ernie Banks (ss) 1958-59
Roger Maris (of) 1960-61
Mickey Mantle (of) 1956-57
Dale Murphy (of) 1982-83

14. Lou Boudreau (Cleveland, 1948) was twenty-four. Boudreau was also the last player-manager to win a pennant.

15. In 1976 Joe Ferguson had only one pass intercepted out of 151 throws.

16. Al Kaline was nineteen when he won it in 1955; Ted Williams was thirty-nine when he won in 1958.

17. Pope John XXIII

18. Jim Braddock

19. Bud Abbott and Lou Costello. They were inducted for their great comedy skit "Who's on First?"

20. Boston Red Sox—thirteen (as of 1987)

21. Felix "Doc" Blanchard

22. Eddie Gaedel was a midget who was sent into a game as a pinch hitter for the St. Louis Browns in 1949. His number was $1/8$. Gaedel walked in his only appearance. The League banned him the next day.

23. Johnny Gee, a pitcher for the New York Giants in the mid-1940s, was six feet, nine inches.

24. George Halas

25. Hoyt Wilhelm

26. The major league record for playing with one team for the most consecutive years is shared by two Hall of Famers, each of whom played with the same team for twenty-three years. Name them.

27. Who was the only man to box both Rocky Marciano and Muhammad Ali?

28. Who was the youngest player to get a base hit in a major league game? Who was the oldest?

29. Who was the oldest player to win an MVP award in major league baseball?

30. Name the only boxer to knock Jake LaMotta down.

31. Who was the oldest player to win a Cy Young Award?

32. Several batters have hit two grand-slam home runs in a single game. One of these was a pitcher. Name him.

33. Which player played the most seasons in the NFL?

34. Who is the only pitcher to hit a grand-slam in a World Series game?

35. Six players have hit home runs in a World Series for teams in each league. Who are they?

36. What NFL player holds the lifetime record for field goals?

37. Who is the only major league pitcher to win two hundred games in his career but not win twenty in any season?

38. What number did Ty Cobb wear as a Detroit Tiger?

39. What NFL quarterback attempted the most passes in his career?

40. Here's an Alabama question. Five players born in Alabama have hit 350 or more lifetime home runs. Who are they?

26. Carl Yasztremski (Boston Red Sox); Brooks Robinson (Baltimore Orioles)

27. Archie Moore, who lost both bouts

28. Tommy Brown of the Brooklyn Dodgers was sixteen; Minnie Minoso of the Chicago White Sox, fifty-three.

29. Willie Stargell of Pittsburgh was thirty-nine when he won it in 1979.

30. Danny Nardico, in the seventh round, on December 31, 1952

31. Gaylord Perry was forty when he won it in 1978 with San Diego.

32. Tony Cloninger of the Atlanta Braves

33. George Blanda—twenty-six (1949-75)

34. Dave McNally of the Baltimore Orioles

35. Roger Maris (Yankees and Cardinals); Johnny Mize (Cardinals and Yankees); Enos Slaughter (Cardinals and Yankees); Bill Skowron (Dodgers and Yankees); Frank Robinson (Reds and Orioles); Reggie Smith (Red Sox and Cardinals)

36. Jan Stenerud—373 lifetime field goals

37. Milt Pappas

38. Trick question! Cobb never wore a number. He retired in 1928, and numbers first appeared in 1929.

39. Fran Tarkenton—6,467

40. Henry Aaron, Willie Mays, Willie McCovey, Billy Williams, Lee May

41. This Hall of Famer hit 399 career home runs but never hit more than twenty-nine in a single season. Who is he?

42. What NFL quarterback had the most career completions?

43. There was one player who appeared in all of the following games:

   a) Don Larsen's perfect World Series no-hitter;

   b) Rocky Colavito's four home-run game;

   c) Willie Mays's four home-run game.

   Name him.

44. Only one team has had three players hit forty or more home runs in one season. Which team, and who were the players?

45. What NFL quarterback had the most consecutive games with at least one touchdown pass?

46. Since 1901 there have been thirteen .400 hitters. Roger Hornsby and Ty Cobb did it three times each. George Sisler hit .400 twice. The others were Nap Lajoie, Joe Jackson, Harry Heilmann, Bill Terry and Ted Williams. How many of these great hitters led their teams to the pennant in a .400 year?

47. Excluding Joe Jackson, who was banned from baseball, what player since 1900 has the highest career batting average without being in the Hall of Fame?

48. What is the longest punt in NFL history?

49. What pitcher holds the record for the most wild pitches in a career?

50. What is the fewest number of games won by a Cy Young Award winner?

51. When was the first televised football game?

41. Al Kaline

42. Fran Tarkenton—3,686

43. None other than former manager Billy Martin

44. The 1973 Atlanta Braves; Henry Aaron (43), Darryl Evans (41), Davey Johnson (40)

45. Johnny Unitas

46. None

47. Frank (Lefty) O'Doul, with a career average of .349 over fifteen years

48. Ninety-eight yards, by Steve O'Neal of the New York Jets on September 21, 1969

49. None other than the knuckle-balling ex-Brave, Phil Neikro. He threw 207 wild pitches.

50. Six—Bruce Sutter in 1979 and Rollie Fingers in 1981 each won six games. Of course, they were both relief specialists.

51. Fordham versus Waynesburg, 1939

52. In 1961 Roger Maris set the all-time single-season home run record with sixty-one. How many intentional walks did he receive that year?

53. Johnny Cooney, a former Boston Brave outfielder, played twenty-two seasons in the major leagues. In that long career he hit two home runs. What is ironic about that fact?

54. What coach coached the longest in the NFL?

55. What unique batting distinction is shared by the following players:

    Buddy Bell (1979), Ralph Garr (1973), Matty Alou (1970), Lou Brock (1967), Maury Wills (1962) and Joe Moore (1935)?

56. Who holds the record for the most lifetime fumbles in the NFL?

57. Only once in major league history were there two triple-crown winners in the same year. The year was 1933. Who were these players, and what else was ironic about their achievement?

58. Who is the only pitcher to start an All-Star game for each league?

59. What boxer had the most fights without a loss?

60. Three pitchers have tossed no-hitters in each league. Who are they?

61. Nicknames have always been a part of baseball. Can you identify the following:
    - a) "Dixie"—Outfielder, Brooklyn and Pittsburgh (1940s and '50s)
    - b) "The Mad Russian"—Outfielder, Chicago Cubs (late 1940s)
    - c) "Plowboy"—Pitcher, Yankees (1950s)
    - d) "Slats"—Shortstop, Cardinals (1940s and '50s)
    - e) "The Hondo Hurricane"—Outfielder and pitcher, Giants (1950s)
    - f) "The Barber"—Pitcher, Giants and Dodgers (1940s and '50s)
    - g) "Jungle Jim"—Outfielder, White Sox (1950s)?

52. None

53. They both came in the same season.

54. George Halas—forty seasons

55. They are the only players to get two hundred or more hits in a season and fail to hit .300.

56. Roman Gabriel—105

57. Both players, Jimmy Foxx of the Athletics and Chuck Klein of the Phillies, were in the same city— Philadelphia.

58. Vida Blue (A's and Giants)

59. Edward Henry Greg—176 (117 no decisions)

60. Denton (Cy) Young, Nolan Ryan and Jim Bunning

61. a) Fred Walker
    b) Lou Novikoff
    c) Tom Morgan
    d) Marty Marion
    e) Clint Hartung
    f) Sal Maglie
    g) Jim Rivera

62. Who was the youngest boxer to win a world title?

63. Who was Floyd Geibell?

64. Who held the heavyweight crown the longest?

65. What boxer had the most career knockdowns?

66. What player had the longest name in baseball history?

67. Who was the tallest pro boxer of all time?

68. Name the only heavyweight champ who was never defeated?

69. Who was the oldest man to win the heavyweight championship?

70. Who said the following:

    a) "Nice guys finish last."

    b) "The Giants is dead."

    c) "Do not alibi bad hops. Anyone can field good hops."

    d) "Hit 'em where they ain't."

    e) "Can't anybody here play this game?"

62. Wilfred Benitez, who was seventeen and a half when he won the light welterweight crown

63. This is one of my favorite trivia questions. Geibell was a pitcher for the Detroit Tigers in 1940, but there is more. In 1940 Detroit led Cleveland in the pennant race by two games with three to play. The final series of the year had Cleveland playing at Detroit. All the Tigers had to do was win one of three games to take the flag.

    In order to try for the sweep, Cleveland planned to use the great Bob Feller on Friday and come back with him on Sunday. Feller had already won twenty-seven games. Detroit's manager Del Baker had three outstanding pitchers, Schoolboy Rowe, Bobo Newsome and Tommy Bridges. Baker decided not to use any of them against Feller in that first game and to save his best for the last two games when Feller would not be the opposing pitcher or when he'd be more tired. So, apparently conceding the first game, the Tigers threw in a raw rookie to face Feller. His name? Floyd Geibell.

    As irony would have it, Geibell was almost perfect that day. He shut out the Indians. Detroit won 2-0 and clinched the American League flag.

64. Joe Louis—eleven years, 252 days

65. Archie Moore

66. 1950s and early '60s pitcher for many teams, including the Cubs and Phillies, Calvin Coolidge Julius Ceasar Tuskahoma McLish. He was known as "Cal." A close second goes to former San Francisco Giants third baseman Alan Mitchell Edward George Patrick Henry Gallagher.

67. Gogea Mitu—seven feet, four inches (327 pounds)

68. Rocky Marciano

69. Jersey Joe Walcott—thirty-seven years, five months, eighteen days

70. a) Leo Durocher
    b) Charley Dressen
    c) Joe McCarthy
    d) Wee Willie Keeler
    e) Casey Stengel

Super Stumpers

If you can answer any ten of the following twenty-five questions, you get your Ph.D. in trivia.

1. Name the military academy featured in the 1981 movie *Taps*.

2. Who created Coca-Cola?

3. What is Donald Duck's automobile tag number?

4. Who is Ramon Estevez?

5. What was the name of the nun in the 1957 movie *Heaven Knows Mr. Allison*?

6. Who played the part of the killer in the movie *Dial M for Murder*?

7. Name singer Johnnie Ray's only movie.

8. Name the saloon where John Wayne was killed in *The Shootist*.

9. What was Mrs. Miniver's first name?

10. What was singer Gene Austin's theme song?

11. Who was Nancy Drew's adopted mother?

12. Can you name Marcus Welby's boat?

1. Bunker Hill

2. Dr. John S. Pemberton

3. 313

4. Real name of actor Martin Sheen

5. Sister Angela

6. Grace Kelly

7. *There's No Business Like Show Business* (1954)

8. The Acme Saloon

9. Kay

10. "My Blue Heaven"

11. Mrs. Hannah Gruen

12. The *Mary D.*

13. What TV character was from Mill Valley, California?

14. Name Ma and Pa Kettle's horse

15. What was President Grant's favorite drink?

16. On the *Mary Tyler Moore Show*, what was Mary's father's occupation?

17. Who was the first winner of the Cy Young award?

18. Who was Paul Bunyan's son?

19. Name Judge Roy Bean's saloon.

20. Who was Buz Sawyer's best friend?

21. What was Secret Agent X-9's real identity?

22. Who was the policeman buddy of Philo Vance?

23. Name the U.S. Coast Guard song.

24. Who was the third child of Adam and Eve?

25. What tennis player has won more Wimbledon titles than anyone else?

13. B. J. Hunnicutt on M*A*S*H

14. Emma

15. Old Crow

16. Doctor

17. Don Newcombe in 1956

18. Jean

19. The Jersey Lily

20. Roscoe Sweeney

21. He was known only as Mr. Corrigan.

22. Sergeant Ernest Heath

23. "Semper Paratus"

24. Seth

25. Billie Jean King